Gifted & Talented Learners

Gifted & Talented Learners

Creating a Policy for Inclusion

Barry Hymer with Deborah Michel

David Fulton Publishers
London
in association with the National Association for Able Children in Education

David Fulton Publishers Ltd
The Chiswick Centre, 414 Chiswick High Road, London W4 5TF

www.fultonpublishers.co.uk

First published in Great Britain in 2002 by David Fulton Publishers
Reprinted 2003
10 9 8 7 6 5 4 3 2

Note: The right of Barry Hymer to be identified as the author of this work has been asserted by him
in accordance with the Copyright, Designs and Patents Act 1988

Copyright © Barry Hymer 2002

British Library Cataloguing in Publication Data
A catalogue record for this book is available from the British Library.

ISBN 1-85346-955-6

Designed and typeset by Kenneth Burnley, Wirral, Cheshire
Printed and bound in Great Britain by Ashford Colour Press Limited, Gosport, Hants.

Contents

Acknowledgements

I am grateful to a number of people for their support and assistance while preparing and writing this book:

David Fulton and his team for their interest in the book at the time of its conception, and for their advice and support during its gestation.

Deborah Michel, my gifted and talented friend and colleague, who consistently challenges educational orthodoxies from first principles. This book is the product of our many discussions, musings and arguments. Deborah was the primary author of Chapter 4: any moments of lucidity can be attributed to her thinking; any lapses in writing style to mine.

Roger Sutcliffe, Jenny Smith, Rick Lee, Mike Sheridan, Simon Beswick, Elaine Jackson, Ann Kendrick and Sarah Ogden, for their contributions to Chapter 5.

Robin Adams and his wonderful class of Key Stage 3 students at the Barrow Pupil Referral Unit. They enticed a middle-aged man into playing football after their weekly philosophy sessions, thereby ensuring a ruptured Achilles tendon and eight uninterrupted weeks with his books and an open computer for company.

Mason Minnitt and colleagues at the Barrow Community Learning Partnership (BCLP) for their support and forbearance during my enforced absence from the office.

My extraordinary wife and children, for coping so intelligently with my immobility and its attendant frustrations.

My gifted and talented parents, Meg and Eric Hymer, to whom this book is dedicated.

BARRY HYMER
March 2002

Foreword

There are those of us who hold fast to core comprehensive values – in which each member of wise, humane, creative, high-achieving and inclusive learning communities is accorded equal worth. We will find the philosophy and practice explored and espoused within this book a confirmation of these values.

There are those of us who subscribe to the notion that an arbitrary percentage of 5–10 per cent of a school population can be labelled as gifted and talented and nurtured accordingly. We are likely to find this a much less comfortable read.

Barry Hymer – ably supported by Deborah Michel, and drawing on the experience and expertise of many teachers, students and researchers – has rigorously examined an essential paradox. 'Why do we cling to a narrow, elitist view of the "gifted and talented" in the face of overwhelming evidence about the wide and rich distribution of gifts and talents demonstrated both within and beyond the formal curriculum?'

As a child in rural Nottinghamshire I remember a friend whose inability to learn anything beyond the three times table was more than counterbalanced by his ability, as a young teenager, to diagnose mechanical faults, and to strip down, repair and reassemble agricultural machinery. In terms of conventional schooling he was in the 5 per cent of least able students academically. As teachers, many of us have worked with countless students whose gifts and talents may be revealed unexpectedly – or may often remain hidden through lack of nurturing, coaching, encouragement or celebration of the small steps on the often arduous road to outstanding success. Often these latent gifts and talents are given expression through the intervention of teachers, whose own gifts and talents extend beyond a passion for sharing their subjects and methodology to encompass the positive harnessing of interpersonal and intrapersonal skills. A warm, demanding teacher who is able to model effective practice, establish positive relationships and boost self-esteem and motivation will blast a huge hole in the 5–10 per cent school 'target group'. As a secondary head teacher in Cumbria I was awestruck by the almost magical change in the quality of art produced by successive cohorts of students taught by a newly arrived and outstanding teacher. When almost 50 per cent of the students in all ability option groups achieve A* or A at GCSE, something special is happening. When male students eschew paintings of tractors, sports cars and heavy metal posters in favour of intricate silk paintings inspired by the patterns of nature – something special is happening.

This book is the start of a new journey for those of us working in the Barrow Community Learning Partnership. It contains many difficult questions – and no easy answers. It draws on a strong research base and questions many assumptions, including those which have informed current education policy. It is certainly a book for everyone whose scepticism is alive and kicking – but also a book for all of us who want to engage in the debate about raising achievement within an inclusive context. Most importantly it is a book which demonstrates that practitioners – and the students we work with – have much to offer as we chart new and more effective pathways through the rapidly evolving twenty-first-century learning landscape.

MASON MINNITT
Director, Barrow Community Learning Partnership (Education Action Zone)
March 2002

THE NATIONAL ASSOCIATION FOR ABLE CHILDREN IN EDUCATION
NACE National Office, PO Box 242
Arnolds Way, Oxford, OX2 9FR

Registered Charity No. 327230

Tel: 01865 861879   **Fax: 01865 861880**

e-mail: info@nace.co.uk   **www.nace.co.uk**

MISSION STATEMENT

NACE . . . the association of professionals, promoting and supporting the education of able, gifted and talented children and young people.

AIMS

1. To promote the fact that able, gifted and talented children and young people have particular educational needs, which must be met to realise their full potential.

2. To be proactive in promoting discussion and debate by raising appropriate issues in all education forums and through liaison with educational policy matters.

3. To encourage commitment to the personal, social and intellectual development of the whole child or young person.

4. To encourage a broad, balanced and appropriate curriculum for the able, gifted and talented.

5. To encourage the use of differentiated educational provision in the classroom through curriculum enrichment and extension.

6. To make education an enjoyable, exciting and worthwhile experience for the able, gifted and talented.

OBJECTIVES

1. To promote the development, implementation and evaluation in all schools and colleges of a coherent policy for the able, gifted and talented children and young people.

2. To provide appropriate support, resources and materials for the education of the able, gifted and talented.

3. To provide methods of identification and support to the education community.

4. To provide and facilitate appropriate initial teacher training and continuing professional development for teachers and school leaders.

5. To facilitate research activities.

1 Overview

1.1 'Their own secret colours.' Gifts known and gifts latent: the challenge of the unexpected

I never thought I was clever, but now I think I might be.
(Student in gifted and talented strand of the DfES Excellence in Cities initiative)

Whatever one believes to be true either is true or becomes true in one's mind.
(John Lilly, *The Centre of the Cyclone*)

At the heart of this book lies my memory of Robert, a ten-year-old boy whom I taught in Hampshire over a decade ago. Robert was a large boy, considered something of a bully by other children, and he was challenging in the classroom. He had moderate generalised learning difficulties and he was functionally illiterate. And a few weeks before the end of the school year, I also discovered he was gifted. Not globally gifted, not outrageously or psychometrically gifted, but still gifted. I discovered his gift by accident. Our school had been participating in the W. H. Smith Poets in Schools scheme, which had brought the poet David Orme ('Mango Chutney') to work with students across the entire Year 5 year group. As one of their poetry-writing exercises, the children had gone out in small groups to explore – in great and close detail – the trees and shrubs adjoining the school's playing fields. They'd reflected, taken notes, drawn observational sketches, seen the trees and leaves and insects in new lights and from new angles, played with language, laughed and had fun. And then they'd returned to the classroom to knock their thoughts, notes, perceptions and reflections into poems. I'd been with Robert and his group throughout their time outside – mostly to manage his tendency to distract others – but back in the classroom my attention was shared with other members of the class. By the time I got around to Robert's desk, he'd managed an illegible sentence, in his typically tight, misspelled and dysfluent script. I asked him what he'd written and there was a long pause as he tried to make sense of his work. Then he replied, in a voice so slow and soft I hardly heard him, 'Even the winter leaves have their own secret colours.'

That was it. One line. But what a line! It was midsummer, and Robert had found and studied a solitary, decaying winter leaf. And in his observations and his slow reflections, Robert captured an image that contained a most deliberate metaphor. He was saying,

I'm convinced, 'Mr Hymer, notice me. I know I've not got a great deal going for me in school, but just sometimes, in some situations, I can do things that will amaze you.' The children's best efforts were collated and published in-house in an anthology entitled, *Their Own Secret Colours*. With the support of David Orme, Robert introduced the anthology to the parents at the official launch. He later told me it was the first time he'd ever been asked to do something important. Robert's moment in the sun coincided with a staggering change in his attitude and performance in school. He saw himself as a poet, as someone who, under the right conditions, could amaze with the power of his words. He still struggled to read and write and acquire new concepts at the speed of his classmates, but the bullying pretty much stopped, the friendships and peer-respect grew and Robert walked around the school and playgrounds with a real, deep and growing sense of self-confidence. He seemed caught up in a virtuous circle. And if that was the effect of Robert's self-perception, who was I to disillusion him? A few weeks later the term and school year ended. I left the school and the area and I've no idea what became of him.

Was Robert really gifted? More specifically, was he a gifted poet? Could one say any more than that *under the right conditions,* he was capable of flashes of poetic inspiration? Does true giftedness rely on the demonstration of gifts over time, if not routinely then certainly on more than one occasion? For myself, I know only that the initial recognition of Robert's achievement had multiple consequences, however temporary. The experience left with me two nagging questions: first, could I ever know a child's potential? And second, if the response to this question were negative (and there'd been nothing in Robert's scholastic, family or psychometric history to lead me to expect a gift for poetry), didn't I have a responsibility to assume that every child had the capacity for exceptional performance? Of course, I wouldn't necessarily know when, to what extent or in which domain of enquiry exceptional performances might arise, but, none the less, I had to allow myself to be surprised more often. And for this to happen, I knew I had in my teaching first to jettison all preconceptions about ability, however defined, and then to strive to create a learning environment rich in intellectual challenge and excitement, safe and emotionally nurturing, and dense in its possibilities for extension – for all my students. It's at this point that the cold sweat of reality intrudes: in what passes for the real world is this possible? I will argue in this short book not only that this is possible (I see gifted teachers doing this time and time again, sometimes against all odds), but that the fruits of recent research about the brain, learning and the needs of learners (including 'gifted and talented' learners) demand that we try.

Questions for discussion

- Can one ever know a child's potential?

- Could a child with generalised learning difficulties seriously be considered gifted?

- Is a truly inclusive approach to gifted and talented education possible – or desirable?

1.2 What are the core values and implications of a truly inclusive approach to gifted and talented education?

The challenge confronting the inclusive school is that of developing a child-centred pedagogy capable of successfully educating all children . . . The merit of such schools is not only that they are capable of providing quality education to all children; their establishment is a crucial step in helping to change discriminatory attitudes, in creating welcoming communities and in developing an inclusive society.

(UNESCO, *Salamanca Statement*, 1994)

I do not believe that the Good Lord plays dice.

(attributed to Albert Einstein)

My experience as Robert's classteacher largely pre-dated my more focused interest in the needs of more able learners, but its memory has resonated strongly whenever I've come across such educational buzzwords as 'inclusion', 'high expectations', 'achievement' or 'underachievement', 'gifted' and 'talented', etc. It seems to me that the challenge posed by Robert is simply a (relatively) extreme example of the dilemma faced by all teachers in the domain of gifted and talented education: how does one create a learning environment that stretches the ablest without excluding or alienating the least able – and vice versa? Any attempt to resolve this question must at some point address issues around core educational principles or values. I will state some of mine here:

- All children have a right to a high quality education.
- The primary aim of education is to excite in children and young people a passion for learning, and to facilitate the acquisition of skills and dispositions which will permit this passion for learning to be satisfied and sustained.
- The primary role of the school is to maximise opportunities for all children to reach their educational goals.
- Children's educational goals will differ.

To these (relatively) uncontroversial principles, the following could be added:

- No-one – not even the person him or herself – is ever fully aware of an individual's potential for learning.
- A fixed concept of 'ability' is an unhelpful descriptor or predictor of performance.
- Children's educational goals are best reached by the setting and answering of questions. These questions are best set by the children themselves.
- Deep learning takes place collaboratively rather than competitively.

Implications of the above would include a recognition that:

- Giftedness and talent are best seen as relative rather than absolute terms, within the context both of an individual child's profile of strengths and weaknesses and his or her wider learning environment.
- The school has an important role in helping *every* child to identify his or her gift/s or talent/s.
- The most effective form of assessment is formative (assessment for learning) rather than summative or normative (assessment for showing or comparing). Relatedly, promoting learning orientation (concern for improving one's learning) is more likely to lead to effective learning than promoting performance orientation (concern for grade success).
- An inclusive policy for gifted and talented education is the only model consistent with these principles.
- The school should take steps actively to implement teaching and learning procedures and methods which will accommodate the principles set out above.

I'm aware that many if not all of the principles and implications set out above are open to challenge, but where values, principles and core beliefs can escape the constraints of subjectivity, a battery of supportive evidence could be cited. This might include, by way of illustration:

- Joan Freeman's comprehensive survey of current international research into the education of able children and young people, in which she concludes that 'The dominant current concern of research into the education of the very able is *the interaction between the child's potential and the provision to develop it*. Without that dynamic element, we return to the old idea of fixed abilities, most notably intelligence' (Freeman 1998:56, italics added). In addition to differentiation, Freeman sees individualisation as the other route to the development of potential – 'Where the pupil has greater responsibility for the content and pace of his or her own educational progress. In this, children would be required to monitor their own learning' (ibid.:56).
- Stephen Ceci's (1990; 1996) and Michael Howe's (1990) robust refutation of the idea that people who excel in certain fields do so because of their special gifts or talents: commitment and practice have been shown to be stronger determinants of exceptional performances than underlying ability.
- Paul Black and Dylan Wiliam's (1998) highly influential report into the key role of formative assessment (or 'assessment for learning') in raising standards in schools.
- Chris Watkins' (2001) extensive review of research evidence suggesting that preoccupation with grade attainment can actually *lower* the quality of performance.
- The growing recognition that thinking and learning are socially regulated activities; social interactions are seen to be essential to such learning processes as voluntary attention, logical memory, concept formation and internalisation. Research in these domains owes a great deal to the writings of the Russian psychologist Lev Vygotsky, but recent applications in the UK educational arena

include Paul Light and Karen Littleton's (1999) demonstration of the significant social and relational bases of learning – even in an age of 'standardised assessment tests' (which are designed to drive up educational standards through the illumination of individual successes and failures).

- The educational implications of the burgeoning body of evidence from cognitive neuroscience. In his review of this area, John Geake has noted that 'There are educational implications here for the measurement of school success as a function of students' perceived individual successes, regardless of their level of achievement. This is not a call for dumbing-down – in fact, quite the opposite. It is a call for school organisation to even further recognise neurobiologically-driven individual differences in responses to school learning, in order to break the cycle of low competence generating low confidence generating low competence, as well as to minimise underachievement by academically gifted children through boredom with an underchallenging age-normed curriculum' (Geake 2002:7).

- Diane Montgomery's conclusions to the book she edited on *Able Underachievers* (2000), in which she observes that 'All learners need to experience an education which is supportive and valuing, whatever their differences. To achieve this, general education needs to be made more flexible. Access to special provision where it is useful should be based on the principles of inclusion and self-referral and use authentic or performance-based assessment to provide feedback to both learners and teachers. Learners need opportunities to contribute their own views on the value and appropriateness of the education they are receiving' (ibid.:202).

Questions for discussion

- What are *your* core educational principles?

- What are the implications of these principles?

- What do you think is at the heart of achievement: gifts or effort?

- How do your students let you know about what (and how) they're learning?

1.3 Principles into practice: rising tides, labels and all that

First say to yourself what you would be; and then do what you have to do.
(Epictetus, *Discourses*)

Research investigations have failed to discover any inherited or genetic
traits that correspond to the popular notion of a natural gift or talent.
(Michael Howe, *Sense and Nonsense About Hothouse Children*)

Within the Barrow Community Learning Partnership (Education Action Zone) the
opportunity has arisen to explore and test the boundaries and possibilities of the principles outlined in this chapter, and in so doing to attempt to meet the challenge currently
facing all schools and local education authorities: the prosecution of two high-profile
agendas, namely raising achievement and promoting inclusion. While these agendas
can easily chafe against each other, it's both our belief and our experience that these
agendas need not through any natural law be contradictory. Given an enabling policy
framework they can be mutually supportive. This book sets out to chart one such framework, in the hope that schools will choose to accept the contemporary challenge of
setting out to meet the needs of *all* their students through an emphasis on gifted and
talented teaching and learning, rather than through the traditional, superficially attractive and ultimately inadequate approach of test-and-place. The framework is not
intended to be prescriptive, and it is hoped that individual schools and teachers will use
it creatively and flexibly, according to their own needs and circumstances. Certainly
there is no one school within the Barrow Community Learning Partnership that would
claim a monopoly on inclusion and attainment within the parameters of a policy for
gifted and talented education, but there are many that hold these principles dear, and
implement them inventively and authentically. They tend to be schools that recognise
the reality of Professor Joe Renzulli's increasingly well-known maxim, that 'a rising tide
lifts all ships'.

In advocating and setting out the challenges and possibilities of a truly inclusive
school-based vision for gifted and talented education, I feel that it's necessary for me to
identify and to nail a few positions that this book is *not* advancing:

1.   'All children have equivalent predispositions for exceptionality.'
2.   'Achievements in traditional curriculum areas aren't worth celebrating.'
3.   'Extension and enrichment activities which engage only a minority of students to
     the highest levels are necessarily flawed or inadequate.'
4.   'There's merit or moral high-ground to be had in devaluing the concept of gifted-
     ness or talent, or relatedly that this approach owes more to social engineering
     ambitions than to social realities.'
5.   'Translating an inclusive policy into practice is easy.'

On the contrary, and sequentially:

1. Of course we're not all born equal. Michael Howe, long-time rebutter of arguments for genetic determinism in the field of giftedness, qualifies his assertion about the lack of research evidence for genetic explanations for natural talent by going on to make the point that '. . . it would be totally wrong to conclude that all infants are born identical, so far as the possible precursors of ability differences are concerned. There do exist early differences between infants, some of which are probably inborn and possibly inherited, that can have effects of various kinds on later development' (Howe 1990:112). It's just that the *outcomes* of these differences are neither fixed, nor direct, nor predictable. I would argue that it's only through proclaiming the *universality* of individual difference and extraordinariness (realised or latent) that it's possible to deny the equivalence of children's diverse range of aptitudes, gifts and talents without being charged with elitism. At the highest levels of achievement, to suggest that Einstein's giftedness was equivalent to Picasso's (or vice versa) and distinguished only by the domain of achievement seems to me to be absurd and irrelevant and betrays our twentieth-century fixation with ranking and measuring the unrankable and unmeasurable. At more modest, school-based levels, to suggest that Paul's giftedness is equivalent to Clare's (whatever these respective gifts might be) seems equally unhelpful.

2. In identifying, nurturing and celebrating the limitless diversity of these gifts and talents it's very easy to include the achievements of the girl who attains twelve A* GCSE grades as one manifestation of giftedness.

3. For a carefully crafted extension activity to engage students at the same level of intensity seems to me to be unlikely: the extent to which we are attracted to different domains of enquiry is a question of degree. Who among us would be equally drawn to investigations around membrane-theory and the prospect of parallel universes, the future of the Internet, the dark underbelly of Victorian London, and the implications of the Quaker phrase, 'Speaking truth to power'? But who among us would have *no* interest in learning *something* about each of these areas?

4. To the suggestion, which I'm sensitive to, that a truly inclusive approach to gifted and talented education so devalues and dilutes the concept of giftedness and talent that it makes the domain meaningless, I would say simply that I have no interest in the term gifted and talented as a form of tattoo, to be etched into the skins of Our Few, Our Precious Few. Labels, even culturally positive labels, do not of themselves lead learning; they are more likely to limit it. But as a signpost to deep, passionate and authentic learning, the term giftedness and talent may well be a rich marker when it's unbounded by quotas or auras of exclusivity – and well worth pursuing on behalf of Our Many. Neither is this an approach which is in the first instance about social engineering or political correctness: of much greater interest to most teachers are the pragmatic considerations of effectiveness and usefulness. I happen to believe that the evidence suggests that inclusive models work better than exclusive models. If at the same time the social improvements described in the *Salamanca Statement on Special Needs Education* can be supported, then so much the better.

5.   It was never going to be easy. Nor can the adoption of an inclusive conception of giftedness and talent be an argument for complacency, a sense that 'We already provide well for our gifted and talented students because our examination results are good.' If anything, as all reflective teachers know, the process of planning, implementing and rigorous reviewing that inclusion requires demands much greater powers of observation, thought and reflection than traditional models of test-and-place or test-place-test. The challenge of true inclusion is a stiff challenge, which can make the relative ease of providing something different for the few very alluring. This is not a new insight. In her thoughtful account of *Clever Children in Comprehensive Schools*, Auriol Stevens (1980) foreshadows the attractions of separate and different educational experiences that are embodied in, for instance, the UK's emerging academy for gifted and talented youth: 'The task is hard. It is made infinitely harder by setting up alternative systems to "save" the clever by taking them out of the common schools. The problem may appear to have been solved by such means, but it will not have been. Attention will simply have been diverted from undertaking the detailed, painstaking work that raising standards for all requires' (ibid.:164).

Two further reflections from the chalkface of exceptionality: in her exploration of the author J. K. Rowling's attitude towards children, Ruth Moore, Chair of the National Association of Teachers of English, made an implicit reference to the 'rising tide' approach when she observed that 'what J. K. Rowling reminds us of very clearly is that every ordinary child is capable of extraordinary achievement. What we have to remember is that every ordinary teacher is capable of helping them to achieve it' (*Times Educational Supplement*, 1 Feb. 2002, *Curriculum Special: English*:4). And in a recent edition of *NAGC News*, the newsletter of the National Association for Gifted Children, the mother of a gifted primary-aged girl writes: 'We are lucky. Nicola is at a school where all children are seen as unique human beings, with gifts and potential waiting to be developed' (*NAGC News*, Jan./Feb. 2002:17). Universality *and* the recognition of individual difference, met by flexibility and differentiated challenge. Now isn't *that* what inclusion's all about?

Questions for discussion

*   Are the Standards and the Inclusion 'Agendas' compatible?

*   Is there value in ranking gifts? Under what circumstances?

*   Does the concept of inclusion devalue the term giftedness?

2 Who is gifted?

Issues around models and definitions of giftedness

2.1 Defining giftedness and talent

> 'Cheshire-Puss,' she began, rather timidly . . . 'Would you tell me, please, which way I ought to go from here?'
> 'That depends a good deal on where you want to get to,' said the cat.
> 'I don't much care where . . .', said Alice.
> 'Then it doesn't matter which way you go,' said the cat.
>
> (Lewis Carroll, *Alice in Wonderland*)

Robust, reliable and educationally authentic definitions of giftedness and talent are elusive. Consider the following fairly traditional definition of giftedness/high ability, from an LEA policy drawn up in 1996: 'The term "more able student" is taken to apply to that individual who is consistently functioning at a level two or more years in advance of the majority of his or her same-age peers – in at least one area of the formal curriculum' (Cumbria Education Service Policy Document for More Able Students, 1996). As the person responsible for recommending this definition for adoption at that time, I feel reasonably entitled to discuss its strengths and its limitations, as I now see them. Its strengths include its eschewal of the need for additional standardised testing (additional to that which is already built in to national measures of achievement), the fact that it's relatively explicit about its client-group, that it requires all schools to recognise that they will have more able students on their roll, and that it is fairly teacher-friendly.

This definition's weaknesses, however, are serious. These include its failure to include within it the needs of the underachieving student, its failure to take account of age-within-grade effects (is a 14-year-old performing at the level of an 'average' 16-year-old really as able as a four-year-old performing at the level of an 'average' six-year-old?) and its limp acceptance of the knowledge-based formal curriculum (and the attendant forms of assessment) as being the only legitimate domain for the expression of exceptional achievement. Moreover, it is at heart a complacent definition that sets few incentives and offers no real signposts to a school wishing to walk that bit further, to move beyond a recognition of existing high-level performances and to work towards the demonstration of high achievement in its many forms for all its students. (It's to the credit of many Cumbrian schools that they chose not to be constrained by the county-definition which we adopted as a 'good-enough' starter. A consortium of schools in the Millom area, for instance, adopted two definitions, one of which resembled the county-definition and another: 'Those students who show an exceptional talent or gift. This might be in a curriculum area or a less easily acknowledged talent such as leadership, social maturity or creative imagination.')

Consider also this staggeringly bold and decidedly questionable definition of giftedness, from a popular book on children's development, written for parents: 'A gifted child is one who has advanced cognitive (understanding) skills and motor skills for her age. She can walk, talk and reason earlier than average. She will be a high achiever in most areas and she may have an IQ over 150' (Stoppard 1995:251). Interesting that this definition would exclude some of the most gifted individuals of all ages, including late talkers (such as John Stuart Mill), countless prodigies who were also late walkers, and legions of late-achievers and creators. Some research has even found that there is *no* discernible relationship between giftedness in young children and advanced motor skills (Robinson 2000). Or consider the equally troubling assertion about the nature of intelligence: 'Intelligence is wholly innate and overrides all cultures and backgrounds; cleverness is partly innate and partly environmental' (Stoppard 1995:251). Really? Even when no less an authority than the psychologist Howard Gardner concludes from the weight of biological research evidence that 'it is impossible to separate out genetic from environmental factors' (Gardner 1997:35)? Yet beliefs about the genetic heritability of intelligence, *as defined by IQ*, remain powerful influences on social policy in our society – and they would be even more powerful if the implications of arguments in books such as Herrnstein and Murray's *The Bell Curve* (1994) were pursued to their dismal ends. We'd do well to remember, however, that assertions about intelligence, cleverness, gifts and talents are only true when our definitions make them so, and we should perhaps be cautious in assuming that our definitions capture the solitary 'truth' out there.

Cheshire Education Service in its *Management Guidelines* (1996) noted that 'There are difficulties in adopting any definition as part of working practice' (p. 6), and almost every authority in the field makes related acknowledgements as to the difficulties inherent in the adoption of any one definition. The House of Commons Education and Employment Committee, in its influential 1999 report on *Highly Able Children* identified the definition of their target group as being the most complex aspect of their inquiry. Joan Freeman has said that 'Arguments about precise definitions and the identification of such children have been active for nearly a century, and will doubtless continue' (Freeman 1998:1). The reason for our inability to arrive at an agreed definition of giftedness and talent is straightforward: gifts and talents, like the sister concept intelligence, elude simple measurement – as do all the best things in life. And while we usually try to ignore that which we cannot measure, gifts and talents are difficult to ignore – so we persist in our utilitarian search for ever more 'accurate' ways of measuring them.

For all the twentieth-century attempts to pin intelligence, giftedness or talent down to a number and to give that number a place on a statistical bell curve, individuals' exceptional achievements have insisted on popping out at every point on that curve and beyond it. The closest it seems we came to nailing the beast/s in an age of positivism was to adopt purely circular definitions, as in E. G. Boring's (1923) 'Intelligence is what intelligence tests test' or in apparently more plausible and contemporary (albeit unattributed) educational terms, 'A more able/gifted child is one who achieves at or above Level 5 in a core subject at the end of Key Stage 2.' And what do definitions like these tell us about all those children who could have reached Level 5 but didn't? Is giftedness captured only in the performance, or in the potential too? And what about those who could have reached Level 5 in empathy, or leadership, or canoeing? Is giftedness really defined by the domain? Then who lays down the value of the domain? And even for the achieving, domain-bound few, do we really know where we as teachers should be going now with the child, and how, and with whom? These and related issues led the researchers Treffinger and Feldhusen (1996) to go so far as to describe the generic term 'gifted' as 'indefensible'. It is, however, the currently dominant term in education in most Western societies, and we need therefore to work around it and embrace it for what it *can* offer. If nothing else, we are forced to confront the fact that intelligence, giftedness and talent – in whatever form – cannot exist in the child alone. Complexity comes in many shades.

Questions for discussion

- Should a definition of giftedness be measurable?

- Is giftedness the same as high intelligence?

- Is giftedness the same as high achievement?

2.2 Towards greater inclusion: defining more widely

I believe in standardising automobiles, not human beings.

(attributed to Albert Einstein)

No more fiendish punishment could be desired, were such a thing physically possible, than that one should be turned loose in society and remain absolutely unnoticed by all the members thereof.

(William James, *The Principles of Psychology*)

Consider these secondary teachers' responses to the question, 'How would you define giftedness in a student?' The constructs or attributions listed in parentheses are my own attempts to capture their essence:

Ability to mentally imagine, calculate and think about problems in depth [*abstract reasoning, visualisation, creativity, processing*]

Natural ability – i.e. can do things very quickly and finds most things easy to understand [*heredity, processing speed*]

Can communicate at sophisticated levels [*communication and social skills*]

Works at a standard far above his peers [*attainment*]

An ability to learn and meet cognitive and intellectual demands through the application of current knowledge, understanding and intellectual skills [*application, problem-solving*]

Subject ability markedly superior to individual's overall ability across subjects [*uneven profile of abilities*]

Depends upon year-group. Also includes abilities other than academic – but we don't tend to see those during lessons [*relative to social context, breadth of definition*]

Ability to think laterally [*creativity*]

A student that can think, work and research independently [*self-reliance and research skills*]

Excellent application of skill and takes risks [*application, resilience*]

One who is able continually and sustainably to show a high level of process knowledge and empathy with other cultures and social groupings [*performance over time, process and socio-emotional skills*]

The student who takes an instruction or idea, sticks with it, and develops it several stages beyond normal expectation [*persistence, creativity, initiative*]

(Staff of Parkview School, Barrow-in-Furness – responses to pre-INSET questionnaire)

Even from the restricted sample of comments listed above, it is clear that these teachers' combined beliefs about the richness and diversity of giftedness go far beyond the easy certainties of more dated conceptions – which often spring from medical models. In an attempt to capture something of the great complexity and richness of the concept of giftedness and talent, a number of complex and rich theories and models have been developed. From the University of Connecticut for instance, Joseph Renzulli's much-quoted three-ring conception of giftedness, which conceptualises highly productive people as having three interlocking clusters of ability, is shown in Figure 2.1.

For Renzulli (1977; 1990), above average (not necessarily exceptional) ability is necessary but not sufficient for giftedness to emerge. Also necessary are the sister-qualities of task commitment (perseverance, endurance, application, practice, self-confidence, openness to constructive criticism, etc.) and creativity (fluency, flexibility and originality of thought, openness to experience, playfulness, etc.). The model has been refined

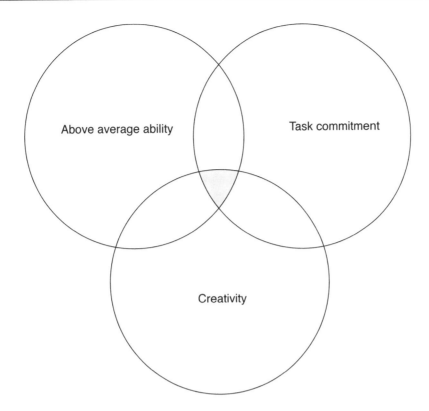

Figure 2.1 Renzulli's three-ring model of giftedness

and developed over time by Renzulli himself and also by those anxious to include not only the *within-child* but also the contextual determinants of giftedness – e.g. the influences of the family, the peer-group and the school (Mönks 1992). At the heart of Renzulli's conception is his notion of *school-wide enrichment* activities, so that all students have the chance to discover their interests, gifts and talents. Renzulli's model has provided the framework for the creation of many insightful and challenging educational opportunities for children, e.g. Holland Park School's provision for gifted and talented learners within the DfES's Excellence in Cities initiative (Warwick 2001).

The two currently most influential theories of intelligence in the disciplines of education and psychology are those of the Harvard and Yale academics Howard Gardner and Robert Sternberg respectively. Gardner's theory of multiple intelligences (Gardner 1983) blew wide open received and deeply rooted conceptions of the nature of intelligence when it first appeared. Through an extensive and multidisciplinary analysis of empirical evidence, and based on a set of eight criteria, Gardner posited the existence of not one unitary notion of intelligence (the theory underpinning the construction and use of IQ tests), but seven relatively discrete intelligences: verbal-linguistic, logico-mathematical, spatial, musical, bodily-kinaesthetic, interpersonal and intrapersonal (Figure 2.2). To these have since been added naturalistic intelligence, and explorations are continuing into the existence of a possible ninth – existential intelligence. Though it has met some resistance and challenge to its theoretical validity in academic circles (notably from those psychologists wedded to the more traditional and 'measurable' conception of a unitary intelligence), multiple intelligences theory has been particularly

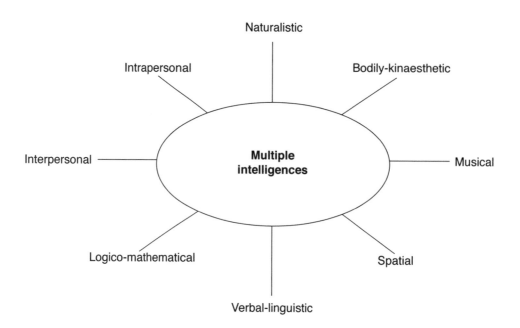

Figure 2.2   Gardner's multiple intelligences

well-received in the world of education, where it has been used as the framework for many creative classroom-based applications (e.g. Lazear 1994a; Haggerty 1995; Marks-Tarlow 1996; Bellanca 1997; Teacher Created Materials 1999).

Robert Sternberg's Triarchic Theory of Intelligence posits the existence of three inter-related subtheories (what he terms the componential, experiential and contextual subtheories) and three aspects of intelligence: analytical, creative and practical (Sternberg 1986). For Sternberg, analytical ability (which is the core component of traditional measures of intelligence) is not enough – the ability to crack abstract logical puzzles, often at speed, is poorly correlated with the ability to crack problems and challenges in the real world. Yet, Sternberg observes, students with strong memories and analytical abilities 'score' at every point in the educational system, both in the organisation of teaching and in the assessment of learning, with the result that certain career paths become barred to differently talented individuals (Sternberg 1997). Sternberg's alternative definition of giftedness reflects his theory:

> Giftedness can come in several varieties. Some gifted individuals may be particularly adept at applying the components of intelligence, but only to academic types of situations. They may thus be 'test smart' but little more. Other gifted individuals may be particularly adept at dealing with novelty, but in a synthetic rather than an analytic sense: their creativity is not matched by analytic power. Still other gifted individuals may be 'street smart' in external contexts, but at a loss in academic contexts. Thus, giftedness is plural rather than singular in nature.
>
> (Sternberg 1986:9)

In his more recent conceptualisation of the Triarchic Theory of Intelligence, Sternberg introduces the notion of Successful Intelligence (Figure 2.3) as better capturing the full nature of human abilities (e.g. Sternberg and Grigorenko 2000). He sets out to demonstrate not only that conventional conceptions of intelligence are incomplete and inadequate (they account only minimally for the variation in numerous measures of life success), and that they've configured schooling and society in unfortunate ways, but that applications of the broader concept of Successful Intelligence can actually improve people's cognitive abilities and their performances in the classroom and at work. Moreover, he argues that adoption of the concept will result in substantial benefits to individuals, institutions and society (presentation to the British Psychological Society DECP Conference, January 2002).

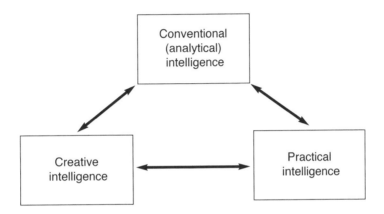

Figure 2.3   Sternberg's concept of Successful Intelligence

While it can be seen that Gardner and Sternberg share similar critiques of conventional conceptions of intelligence, they part ways fundamentally in the extent to which an individual's intelligences are considered to relate to the domains in which they're operating: Sternberg seems to believe that it's relatively immaterial whether a child is processing pictures, words, numbers, space or emotions – the same intellectual facets will be at work. For Gardner, the domain within which a child is working is considered central to the intellectual processes brought to bear on that domain. This seems to underlie Gardner's scepticism about freestanding approaches to, for instance, thinking skills or memory improvement: memorising nouns is a different intellectual challenge from memorising cricket statistics or fugues.

Yet another rich and contextualised conceptualisation of giftedness is Mihaly Csikszentmihalyi's *system view* of creativity and extraordinariness (Figure 2.4). For Csikszentmihalyi (1996), it is necessary to look wider than the individual's brain, mind or personality in order to understand her apparent gifts or talents. It is the interaction between three core elements that is important: the *individual*, with her gifts, talents, goals and values; the *domain* or discipline in which the individual is working; and the *field* of peers, teachers, examiners, experts, etc. who will evaluate and pass judgement on her work. For all its richness, the conceptualisation has its own challenges. Consider for instance the Year 6 child who is a promising mathematician, who has access to extracurricular maths tuition and who excels in the KS2 maths SATs, achieving Level 6. She

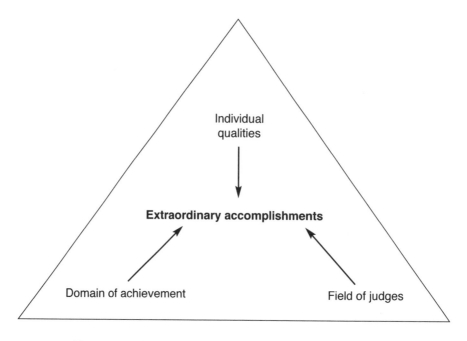

Figure 2.4   Csikszentmihalyi's system view of extraordinariness

could be regarded as gifted in Csikszentmihalyi's terms, whereas the hypothetical class-mate with equivalent mathematical flair but whose parents do not or cannot pay for a private tutor may fail to achieve Level 6. Is he really a less gifted mathematician? Perhaps not in terms of potential, but according to Csikszentmihalyi's system view, he will be a less *extraordinary* mathematician, having failed to satisfy the demands of the field (the SAT examiners) that he merits a Level 6 attainment.

A final conceptualisation of giftedness which must be explored at this stage is that contained in the DfES Excellence in Cities initiative, the Gifted and Talented strand of which is being used as a pilot for a national strategy for gifted and talented students in maintained schools. This can be viewed as embodying a pragmatic but nakedly atheoretical definition of giftedness and talent, although interestingly the accompanying documentation is theoretically well-grounded. Gifted and talented (secondary-aged) students are defined in actuarial rather than qualitative terms as consisting of 5–10 per cent of the overall school population – existing or potential high-achievers. This proportion of students reflects a decision rooted less in social science than in social policy, as does the related requirement for schools to identify their gifted and talented students in ratios of approximately two to one respectively. Gifted students are defined as those having abilities in the core academic subjects, and talented students are defined as those having abilities in the creative and expressive arts and in PE, although it is acknowledged that some students will be both gifted and talented. The gifted/talented distinction is made despite Winner's evidence-based assertion that 'Two different labels suggest two different classes of children. But there is no justification for such a distinction' (Winner 1996:7).

For all its quantitative neatness, the advice informing the Excellence in Cities initiative is at pains to stress the importance of looking widely towards latent or non-academic manifestations of giftedness or talent, and there does seem to be a tension in the twin imperatives: to count what can be counted and to include what can't. Deborah Eyre has noted that although the approach has enjoyed a good deal of success, notably in raising awareness of needs and in fostering creative experimentation with the curriculum, 'the creation of the cohort has been the most problematic aspect of the policy' (Eyre 2001:11).

Questions for discussion

- Which of the four theoretical conceptualisations of giftedness do you like most? Why?

- Do we distinguish between gifts and talents in our society? On what basis, and why?

- How do we communicate the value we place on different gifts and talents?

2.3 In-built inclusion – all gifted?

> Giftedness is something we invent, not something we discover: It is what one society or another wants it to be, and hence its conceptualisation can change over time and place.
>
> (Sternberg and Davidson, *Conceptions of Giftedness*)

> Every child wants to be good at something, and every child can be.
>
> (Joan Freeman, *How to Raise a Bright Child*)

Ellen Winner (1996), whom I invoked in Section 2.2, identified nine myths about giftedness. Her eighth is the assertion that 'All children are gifted'. If this is taken to mean that all children have an equal potential for learning, then we're on sticky ground – manifestly, some children learn new skills and concepts more fluently, more flexibly and more accurately than others. If, however, we take this assertion to mean that every child has one area of relative personal strength, or more than one, then I would claim that the assertion is less of a myth than a defensible truth (albeit one among many competing truths!). Consider this thought experiment:

'Thought Experiment'

A Secretary of State for Education, in some brave new world, defines giftedness as 'the ability to juggle five ping pong balls'. Some children have well-developed motor-skills and eye–hand coordination and they learn this skill quite rapidly. They are tested and identified as gifted and are invited to take part in a daily circus-skills extension workshop. Other children, less naturally dextrous but hugely envious of their classmates' participation in these workshops, develop their skills in remedial sessions after school, practise hard and eventually pass the test necessary to enter the gifted programme. Some children, for all their extra tuition and practice, fail to master the art of juggling five balls, and are denied the extension opportunities. They become disaffected and opt out of juggling experiences, saying that 'juggling is boring' and that 'jugglers are swots'. Some deny the relevance of juggling to their lives, but are reasonably content with other areas of the curriculum. Still others fail at juggling but show an unexpected talent for taming Siberian tigers, but their talents go unrecognised. Over time, inevitably, a whole raft of changes begins to creep into the educational system: parents introduce ping-pong ball mobiles to their infants' cots; health visitors screen for juggling pre-skills at 18 months and three years; the Teacher Training Agency includes juggling skills in its core programme; Standard Assessment Tests of Juggling Proficiency are introduced at Key Stages 1–3; private juggling clinics and juglexia support and pressure groups spring up around the country; therapies based on alternative juggling methods emerge, as does a juggling-skills weakness on chromosome 14 and a proven link between diet and juggling skills. And just as we're priding ourselves on the nation's rising standards of juggling skills (relative to all our juggling competitors), we're invaded by vast packs of Siberian tigers – which ravage our lands and against which our finest jugglers are impotent. A new Secretary of State defines giftedness as 'naturalistic intelligence, especially as demonstrated in engagements with wild cats (stripy variety)'.

If Sternberg and Davidson are right, and giftedness is not discovered but invented to meet a more or less ephemeral social need, would we not do well to keep an open mind about what we value in our society? Defining giftedness in terms of juggling skills – if this is what we currently need and value – may be fine, but let's not neglect our gifted and possibly juglexic tiger-tamers whom we may need in the future – and who themselves need now their moments in the sun.

Within the Barrow Community Learning Partnership we have attempted to come up with a definition of giftedness and talent which eschews traditional conceptions of such terms as 'intelligence', 'ability' and 'giftedness and talent' itself, while retaining something of the richness of less deterministic, more contemporary, dynamic and educationally hopeful conceptualisations – such as those presented in recent decades by Renzulli, Gardner, Sternberg and Csikszentmihalyi. At the same time, we have recognised the need and the advantages for our schools of working substantially within the framework being established nationally in this field of education. Our remit, therefore, was to develop a definition which met the following specifications:

- It should reflect existing and emerging theory and evidence about the antecedents of achievement.
- It should see the challenge of identification as being integral to the challenge of provision.
- It should embrace crucial 'trans-intellective' components of high achievement.
- It should be aspirational at all levels – for students, for parents, for schools, for supporting bodies and institutions (e.g. governing bodies, EAZs, LEAs, etc.) and for wider communities.
- It should be non-discriminatory.
- It should recognise a wide range of abilities, skills, qualities and dispositions, including those which are not currently dominant in our society.
- It should be compatible, in general terms, with the thrust of national initiatives.
- It should set out, in broad, clear but non-prescriptive terms how schools might set about such essential work as identifying and providing for giftedness and talent.
- It should be couched in language that is accessible.

A final specification falls in almost as a secondary gift to those identified above: it should promote inclusion. Given the needs of our community for a definition of giftedness or talent that comes close to meeting the imperatives outlined above, we have come up with the following:

Within the Barrow Community Learning Partnership (BCLP) a gifted or talented student is regarded as one who has

(i) experienced a degree of facilitated self-reflection on his or her pattern of learning strengths and preferences; *and*
(ii) identified his or her area(s) of greatest strength(s) within the framework of an enriched learning environment.

Strengths would include gifts and talents as identified by the DfES Excellence in Cities initiative (Gifted and Talented strand) and also less easily measurable 'soft' skills and qualities such as interpersonal and intrapersonal skills and other elements crucial to thinking for learning (e.g. resilience, analysis, wise judgement and discernment, intuition and imagination).

(Definition for the BCLP Gifted and Talented Policy, January 2002)

Questions for discussion

- Is giftedness really invented, not discovered? Did society invent Mozart or discover him?

- Are very young children capable of reflection?

- Does the definition above meet all the specifications set for it? What are its weaknesses?

3 Who says she's gifted?

Issues around identification strategies

3.1 Identifying for inclusion – identification through provision

> Insanity: doing the same thing over and over again, and expecting different results.
>
> (attributed to Albert Einstein)

> We strive to ensure that all participants have a reasonable chance of victory.
>
> (Entry-form for a race)

In their evaluation of the Excellence in Cities and other grant-funded programmes aimed at providing for gifted and talented students the Office for Standards in Education (Ofsted 2001) identified very many positive outcomes of these programmes. A few areas for concern were also identified, however, and these included the following:

> The identification of gifted and talented students has presented difficulties for schools. To date, methods of identification have generally been rudimentary and have not yet solved the problem of recognising latent high ability, particularly among students who are underachieving generally. (ibid.:3)

> . . . some students not identified clearly felt it unfair that they were excluded from activities and were demotivated as a result. (ibid.:15)

> The Excellence in Cities guidance hoped that the initiative would help to change the approach to curriculum organisation in schools. It was not yet doing so to any significant degree in the schools in the survey. There were as yet few signs of radical changes to the organisation of classes or the curriculum and its teaching. (ibid.:20)

I believe the three concerns are related, and not just a consequence of the fact that the initiative hadn't yet 'bedded down' in the schools. As long as schools are required to focus on identifying only a proportion of their students for inclusion in any 'distinct teaching and learning programme', then inevitably sins of omission and commission will be made – however inadvertently, however fluid the system for students' entering and exiting the gifted and talented cohort, and however complex and comprehensive the raft of identification procedures employed in the school. As long as we adhere to a twentieth-century test-and-place model of identification, then the requirement for schools (and society) to make the 'radical changes to the organisation of classes or the curriculum and its teaching' – where this is needed – will be deferred.

In their report into the relative merits of enrichment or acceleration in mathematics, Tony Gardiner and his colleagues (Gardiner 2000) suggested that the concept of identification is *in itself* unavoidably exclusive and rigid. It is seen to be a poor predictor of future success, with a tendency to distort the development both of those included and of those excluded. It should, they argue, be jettisoned. There is, however, an alternative approach to identification, one which doesn't involve ditching the term altogether. Joan Freeman, in championing an 'identification-through-provision' approach has coined the term 'The Sports Approach'. This approach seeks to consider aptitude and provision simultaneously, not sequentially, and it places less emphasis on the existence of some pre-existent gift or talent than on the following elements:

- Seeing identification as process-based and continuous.
- Basing identification on multiple criteria, including provision for learning and outcome.
- Validating indicators for each course of action and provision.
- Presenting students' abilities as a profile rather than a single figure.
- Adopting increasingly sharp criteria at subsequent learning stages.
- Recognising that attitudes may be affected by outside influences such as culture and gender.
- Involving students in their own educational decision-making, especially in areas of their own interest.

(Freeman 1998:19)

Freeman draws on extensive research findings as inspiration for The Sports Approach, including the findings of the British Sports Council's three-year longitudinal study on the training of young athletes (Rowley 1995). This study examined the origins of children's participation in sport – the people who'd identified their potential, and the reasons for their starting training. It was apparent, as paraphrased by Freeman, 'that the identification of high-level sporting talent was heavily dependent on provision for both tuition and practice, which often depended on parents, as well as on the motivation of the children themselves. Thus, sports clubs and coaches could only play a secondary role in identifying talent, as they could only select already high achievers' (ibid.:16). It is unrealistic, the argument goes, to expect to be able to identify giftedness or talent independently of the provision which makes the flowering of these gifts or talents possible. Until children have access to high-quality, enriched learning opportunities, it is impossible to know with any degree of certainty which children will most benefit from these opportunities. This is of course not to deny that some children, depending on the domain of enquiry and the teaching strategies adopted, will perform at a higher level – but the starting point is fair, equitable and good-for-all.

The adoption of an identification-through-provision model creates its own challenges. While no time need be wasted leafing through the catalogues of suppliers of educational tests in search of the 'ultimate' test, a good deal of thought does need to be given to ways of creating and sustaining an enriched learning environment. And arguably even more thought needs to be given to methods for observing and making sense of the behaviours demonstrated by children working in this environment, in order to plan and differentiate future learning challenges. Observational assessment methods can be informal, relatively record-free and intuitive, or more structured. Perhaps ironically given their rejection of traditional test-and-place models of identification, some observational approaches have even found their way into the test catalogues: a good example is Koshy and Casey's *Special Abilities Scales* (2000), which derive from Renzulli's conceptualisations of giftedness, via implementation in New Zealand and adaptation to the UK system. In this set of observational scales students' characteristics are rated 1 (seldom or never observed) through to 4 (always or almost always observed), and an individual student profile is obtained. This profile consists of the following five scales:

- *Learning characteristics* (e.g. easily grasps underlying principles, problem-finding and -solving, jumping learning stages);
- *Social leadership* (e.g. communicates well in groups, inspires a group to meet goals, actively seeks leadership);
- *Creative thinking* (e.g. produces original ideas, displays intellectual playfulness, imagination and fantasy, isn't afraid to be different);
- *Self-determination* (e.g. expresses ideas and opinions forthrightly, pushes adults for explanations, challenges authoritarian pronouncements);
- *Motivation* (e.g. self-direction, self-critical and evaluative stance adopted, prefers independent work).

It is easy to make the links between these characteristics and Renzulli's three-ring model of giftedness: the 'learning' factors have their rightful place, but they don't dominate.

The Special Abilities Scales are suitable for Key Stages 2 to 4, but more open-ended assessments may be needed for younger children. From Nebraska, an 'authentic' form of observational assessment which is well-suited to children aged four to eight years is the Nebraska Starry Night (Griffin *et al.* 1995). This is best described as a general screening measure, but one which fits well in an inclusive school and an identification-through-provision model. The notion of ability at this age seems secondary to the notion of learning preference, although a correlation is assumed. A wide, creative and sometimes surprising range of learning dispositions is covered, including those behaviours with cognitive, emotional and social components. An interesting example is the constellation of behaviours which is termed 'Act Hunger', covering those children who demonstrate a strong drive to express themselves and be seen, to be enthusiastic and expressive exhibiters, announcers and gesturers! The construction and implementation of the Nebraska Starry Night profile is predicated on the belief that 'Preference profiles, when based on actual child behaviour, can directly influence the learning environment, selection of materials and student learning' (ibid.:40).

Questions for discussion

- Still more change? Do we really need 'radical changes to the organisation of classes or the curriculum and its teaching'?

- Which is easier – 'test-and-provide' or 'identification-through-provision'?

- Which is better – 'test-and-provide' or 'identification-through-provision'?

3.2 Identification through provision: the role of facilitated reflection

Nobody ever learned anything from experience.
It was the reflection on the experience that taught him something.

(Neville West)

There should be brief intervals of time for quiet reflection . . .
used to organise what has been gained in periods of activity.

(John Dewey, *Experience and Education*)

Few are those who see with their own eyes and feel with their own hearts.

(attributed to Albert Einstein)

The definition of giftedness and talent created and adopted within the Barrow Community Learning Partnership, and cited in Section 2.3, embodies two key components: the notion of an enriched learning environment, and the notion of facilitated self-reflection. Both are essential and related, since there is little merit in having students reflecting deeply on their strengths and weaknesses as they come to identify these within a relatively impoverished or even an ordinary learning environment. No child, no matter how great her predisposition to giftedness, becomes gifted without the tools and support of her environment (Howe 1990; Freeman 2001). Possible routes to the creation of an enriched learning environment are discussed in future chapters. Similarly, all the stimulation, challenge and enrichment in the world will have little lasting impact on a child when these experiences are divorced from the sense he or she makes of them: how they are received, configured and internalised, how they are valued and, vitally, how they are used.

The process of reflection is increasingly being seen to be crucial to learning. John Dewey knew this way back. More recently, Howard Gardner has suggested that if one wants to make an impact on a domain or on people, 'one is well advised to engage in regular and searching introspective activities; to locate one's areas of strength and build upon them as much as possible; and, finally, to interpret daily as well as "peak" and "trough" experiences in ways that are revealing rather than defeating' (Gardner 1997:153). Guy Claxton includes reflection as one of the 'three Rs of learning power', alongside resilience and resourcefulness (Claxton 1999). Claxton, invoking Boud (1995) states that in the learning society 'it is more and more up to individuals to assess for themselves what they know, and what they need to know. To be able to monitor and check your own progress; to know when you have done good work; to diagnose your own learning strengths and needs; to develop professional judgement; to take stock of achievement: for all these reasons, the cultivation of the disposition and the ability to self-assess is invaluable' (Claxton 1999:305).

For a school community that is seeking to support all its students in identifying their individual gifts and talents, a number of questions should arise:

- What conceptual model/s for reflection will we adopt?
- How can we model the process of reflection as a school community?
- How can we build opportunities for student self-reflection into the curriculum?
- How can we convert the fruits of reflection into future practice, and encourage our students to do the same?
- How do we ensure that student self-reflection is 'triangulated', so that self-perceptions and insights can be tested against others' perceptions – including those of parents and teachers?

The choice of one or more conceptual models makes the related questions easier to address. Attractive for our purposes is Boud's Reflection Model (Boud *et al.* 1985; Boud and Walker 1990). For Boud, reflection is a normal, ongoing process which can be made more explicit and more ordered. It can only be undertaken by the learner, although it can be facilitated by others, including the teacher. It can be goal-directed, and it is a complex process in which both feelings and cognition are closely interrelated and interactive. Moreover, it is an active process of exploration and discovery that often leads to unexpected outcomes, and it can take place both during and after the experience.

Based on Boud's model, the following exercise in experiential reflection could become a regular part of students' learning experiences. It could be a source of learning growth and support the formation of positive self-concepts. It lends itself to adaptation to suit the needs of children at all Key Stages. Initially, students may find the novelty and lack of fit with 'normal' school experiences amusing, possibly even unsettling – and this is as true for their teachers! As with most exercises of this nature, responses get better and deeper with practice and familiarity, and the formal structure of the script can be loosened over time. Ideally, the students should have some experience of 'stilling' or relaxation exercises. Good resources for developing children's receptivity to reflection and visualisation exercises are exercises to be found in Mary Stone's short book, *Don't Just Do Something – Sit There* (1995), and Jennifer Day's *Creative Visualisation with Children* (1994).

Class Reflection Exercise: identifying my gifts and talents

(Hymer 2002, based on Boud's Reflection Model, 1985)

[*Recommended: soft background music playing; and a 'Do Not Disturb Our Guided Reflection' sign on the classroom door!*]

Read the script below slowly and flexibly, pausing wherever appropriate to permit thinking time, and adding details where these will aid recall and reflection.

Preparation

'I'd like you to put down your pens and books, sit comfortably with your feet on the floor and your back straight but relaxed, and close your eyes. Try to lose any awareness of noises or people alongside you, and breathe in slowly – in through your nose, and out slowly through your mouth. Do this ten times, by yourself. [*Pause.*] We're going to reflect on our own learning today (or this morning/afternoon/week).'

Stage 1 – Returning to experiences

'Remember what you've done today. [*Cue specific activities as appropriate.*] Imagine you've been videoed as you were working, and watch yourself on play-back. Notice things as they happened and how you responded. Notice what you were doing. Notice what was happening elsewhere in the classroom. Which activity did you *really* get into, even if only for a short time? Notice every detail about this activity. Had you done this work before, or was it fairly new? What did it involve? Numbers? Words? Music? Using and moving your body? Finding patterns? Creating something new? Cracking a problem? Were you working alone, or with others? Take a few moments to reflect on this experience.'

Stage 2 – Attending to feelings

'Remember how you felt as you were working. How did your feelings change as you did different things? What feelings did you have? Excited? Bored? Anxious? Absorbed? Restless? Curious? Frustrated? Involved? Now reflect again on the work-activity that you most enjoyed doing. What was it? What did it involve? Did you do it alone, or with others? Pay attention especially to how you *felt* when you were absorbed in this. Think of three words to describe how you felt as you were doing this activity.'

Stage 3 – Associating and re-evaluating the experience

'Now try to connect the feelings and thoughts you had while doing this activity with other times in the past, when you had similar feelings and thoughts. What were these times? How were your *feelings* the same? How were they different? How were your *thoughts* the same? How were they different? At these times, were you busy with the same sort of work-activity, or was it different? How was it the same? How was it different?'

Stage 4 – Integration

'Think now about how you can build a fuller model of yourself as a learner: What did you know about yourself as a learner before today? What do you now know about how you learn best or most enjoyably? Think of one thing that you knew before about how you learn, and one new thing that you know now. What really interests you? Is it a subject as a whole, or a specific activity? Or is it a specific way of working? What is it that you like about this area or way of working? Is it that you feel you're already good at it? Or is it the challenge of getting better at it? Or is it simply that you're interested in it, and get pleasure from it? Or is it something else? Try to build a new model of yourself as a learner, which uses your existing knowledge and your new insights from today. What does the new, learning "you" look like?'

Stage 5 – Validation

'Try now to check out whether you feel comfortable with your new model of yourself as a learner. Does it feel right? Does it fit with what you know about yourself and how you've felt and thought in the past? Does it fit with how others might see you? How could you test out the new learning "you"? Is there anyone you could trust to give you honest feedback? When will you approach them? Are there learning situations in which you check out your new insights and model for yourself? Would these be in school or out?'

Stage 6 – Appropriation

'If you feel already that you've gained a better understanding of yourself as a learner, and that it feels "true", what happens next? How could you use this understanding well? How could you develop your strengths, your learning preferences, your gifts or your talents? Could you use your strengths to get round your weaknesses? How? Could you use your strengths to develop your strengths still further? How could you use your strengths not just for yourself, but for others? For your friends, your class, your school, your family, or your community? Take a few moments to reflect on these things, then, when you feel ready, open your eyes.'

It may be useful, following a class reflection exercise, to ask the students to complete and return a simple pro-forma to the class or form-teacher, which could be used as the basis not only for record-keeping and monitoring, but also for future lesson-planning, implementation and evaluation (including future reflection exercises):

'Fruits of Reflection'

As I understand them so far, I think I have the following gifts and talents:

_____

_____

_____

Ways in which I might be able to develop or find out more about them:

_____

_____

_____

_____

If I'd like an opportunity to discuss these reflections with a teacher, I'll tick this box: ❑

My name: _____ Date: _____

Questions for discussion

- Are there alternative procedures for self-reflection that you yourself use? How could they be applied in the classroom?

- What needs to happen in your class before a class reflection exercise could be tried?

- What happens when students' perceptions of their strengths don't match your own perceptions of their strengths?

3.3 Identification through provision: the role of teachers

A good assessment instrument can be a learning experience. But more to the point, it is extremely desirable to have assessment occur in the context of students working on problems, projects or products that genuinely engage them, that hold their interest and motivate them to do well. Such exercises may not be as easy to design as the standard multiple-choice entry, but they are far more likely to elicit a student's full repertoire of skills and to yield information that is useful.

(Howard Gardner, *Multiple Intelligences: The Theory in Practice*)

Traditional approaches to the identification of gifted and talented children invariably involve some combination of standardised testing of attainment or 'abilities', teacher-nomination, and the use of teacher or parent-completed checklists. While there are many tests and checklists that have been developed for this purpose (cf. Freeman 1998:11–13 for a critique of some of these and for a checklist based entirely on empirical evidence), a truly inclusive approach to identification surrenders prime responsibility for identification to the students themselves – hence the emphasis on such processes as reflection and self-organised learning. It would be unrealistic, however, to expect the teacher to play *no* part in this challenge. Teachers play a crucial role in the foremost challenge – that of creating and sustaining an enriched and stimulating learning environment which gives all students an opportunity to reveal (albeit at different times) their unique profiles of strengths. In this regard Deborah Eyre (2001) sees the school and its teachers' role as being twofold, ensuring both the *range* and the *quality* of provision:

> Range is important because it allows children to discover their talents. A child never introduced to improvised drama is unlikely to know that they have a talent for this . . . The quality of what is offered is equally as important as the range. If schools have low expectations of their children and set tasks accordingly then it is difficult for those with the ability to achieve highly. Equally, if challenging opportunities are always offered to a restricted group then those outside the group are unable to demonstrate high levels of achievement.
>
> (Eyre and McClure, 2001:15)

Teachers also play a critical role in marshalling their observations, intuitions and assessment data in ways that permit patterns and profiles to be discerned, and student-reflections to be examined, clarified, challenged and validated – part of the 'triangulation' necessary to ensure that the fruits of student reflections fit with the available evidence. And since the aim in all of this is to direct and promote learning rather than to categorise individuals' cognitive or learning styles (however seductive and interesting that side-issue may be), of far greater value than pencil-and-paper tests is the careful observation of students engaged in authentic learning experiences: how do students set about managing their resources during a CASE (Cognitive Acceleration through Science Education) lesson? How satisfied are they with a dictionary definition of 'genocide' – does it capture the experiences of victims and killers in the Warsaw Ghetto, Rwanda or Srebrenica? How comfortable are they with the experience of being *stuck* during a maths investigation? Is this a source of humiliation and frustration, or of curiosity and lateral thinking? What is the range of approaches demonstrated by students while engaged in a group problem-solving activity? Role-playing? Discussion? The application of logic and analysis? Sensitivity to others' thoughts and feelings? Looking for patterns, similarities and differences? Howard Gardner (1999), in considering authentic methods of assessing multiple intelligences, makes the interesting point that this could well be achieved by following a group of children around a hands-on, child-centred museum for a morning, but *not* by administering a battery of standardised tests in an office or classroom – for a week. Authentic assessment is indivisibly related to authentic learning – as a formative process rather than as a crystallised, summative state (cf. Hymer *et al.* 2002).

And in making sense of these and other observations, there may well be merit in employing or constructing some explicit assessment framework, especially if this can be co-constructed with the students themselves. Gardner's multiple intelligences theory provides one such framework, and writers such as David Lazear (1994b) and Belle Wallace (2000) have provided a rich menu of techniques for mapping individuals' unique profiles of intelligences in authentic, real-world contexts. Sally Reis and colleagues (1994) have suggested creative ways of eliciting students' interests and areas of expertise when exploring enrichment options as part of a compacted curriculum.

Within the Barrow Community Learning Partnership we have been working on ways of integrating key 'trans-intellective' components of performance with the more traditional domains of ability – as represented for instance by the analytical component of Sternberg's Successful Intelligence and Gardner's verbal-linguistic and logical-mathematical intelligences. This deliberate conflation of such constructs as intelligence, ability, skill, quality and other learning dispositions is discussed in more detail in Chapter 4, but examples of the way(s) in which these dispositions could be elicited from students (peer and self-identification), and then 'mapped' as a contribution to students' profiles of gifts and talents, are provided in the activities outlined below.

'Mrs Fitzwilliam's Legacy'

Aim: to provide a game-based opportunity for students to nominate themselves and their peers for the demonstration of gifts, talents and dispositions.

Appropriate for: students in upper Key Stage 2 and Key Stage 3 as a cross-curricular thinking skills or PSHE/Citizenship exercise, or simplified for younger students.

Organisation: combination of whole-class and mixed-ability small-group (5-8) collaboration.

Duration of exercise: one hour in total.

Procedure
(A) Bring in a mock last will and testament (the usual tea-stained scroll). Explain to the class that Mrs Fitzwilliam, a reclusive widow living in a small bungalow just off (provide a fake address in the vicinity of the school), has died – leaving an unexpectedly large legacy of £475,000. The instructions in her will were unusual: the future of the town depended, she believed, on children developing and using a wide range of qualities. The entire legacy would be left to the group of [ ]-year-old children who between them were able to demonstrate the following qualities (have these available on sets of cards):

- A sense of curiosity and wonder
- An ability to think and act creatively
- An ability to think ahead and predict 'what might be'
- An ability to think logically and elegantly
- An ability to stick at a problem or task in the face of initial failure
- Powers of motivation – for oneself and for others
- Honesty
- A concern for the wider community
- An ability to communicate clearly
- Planning and organising skills
- Independence skills
- Wise judgement – weighing up all factors and deciding carefully
- Teamworking skills
- Sensitivity to others' feelings and thoughts
- Respect for others.

(B) As a whole class, briefly consider each quality in turn, and ensure that all students have at least a reasonable grasp of what each quality means and might look like. Invite them to nominate one member of each group to note-take a spider-gram or mindmap of each quality during this session (with support from other group members). [*10 minutes*]

(C) In groups, ask students to prepare a case to put to the executors of Mrs Fitzwilliam's estate, in which they will argue that each member of their group con-tributes at least one (two or three for smaller groups) of the desired qualities to the whole group. Members representing each quality in turn should be able to provide evidence for their claims which might be challenged by the 'executors' (other members of the class) and supported by other members of the group. The attached record sheet should be completed for each group. [*30 minutes*]

(D) Groups present their cases in turn to the executors (other group members), after which each group must decide how to cast a block vote – groups must vote, but they can not vote for their own group. [*20 minutes*]

Mrs Fitzwilliam's Legacy: Group Record Sheet		

Date: _____

Student Name	*Quality*	*Demonstration of Evidence*
	A sense of curiosity and wonder	[e.g. Adam loves to explore new ideas and possibilities – he plays around with ICT software and discovers new uses for it.]
	An ability to think and act creatively	
	An ability to think ahead and predict 'what might be'	
	An ability to think logically and elegantly	
	An ability to stick at a problem or task in the face of initial failure	
	Powers of motivation – for oneself and for others	
	Honesty	
	A concern for the wider community	
	An ability to communicate clearly	
	Planning and organising skills	
	Independence skills	
	Wise judgement – weighing up all factors and deciding carefully	
	Teamworking skills	
	Sensitivity to others' feelings and thoughts	
	Respect for others	

Learning Dispositions Log

Stimulus lesson: a lesson in any curriculum area which provides opportunities for a wide range of learning dispositions to emerge. Examples of such lessons are provided in Chapter 5.

Learning log: sheet/s distributed to students at the *start* of the lesson. Help orient the class to its structure, and what it aims to do. Ask them to put it aside until the end of the lesson. To avoid overload, especially for younger students, it may be helpful to focus on a limited number of dispositions only (as few as one in the early stages of their exposure to this form of reflection).

Learning Log (Upper KS1–Lower KS2 (for the processing of lesson content)

Name: _____ Date: _____

Write or draw a picture to show when you . . .

Disposition	Item	Example (words or picture)
 (logical and analytical thinking)	. . . worked something out by thinking hard:	
 (creative thinking)	. . . thought of something in a new way:	
 (curiosity and wonder)	. . . asked a 'What if . . . ?' question:	
 (prediction and inference)	. . . thought of what might happen next:	

Disposition	Item	Example (words or picture)
(resilience)	. . . battled on when you were stuck:	
(motivation)	. . . tried to do something really well:	
(honesty)	. . . said when you got something wrong:	
(community/ethics)	. . . did what you thought was right and true:	
(applying prior knowledge and experience)	. . . used something you already knew:	

Disposition	Item	Example (words or picture)
(planning and organisation)	. . . planned well:	
(independence)	. . . worked by yourself:	
(balance/decision-making)	. . . made a hard decision:	
(collaboration)	. . . worked well with others:	
(empathy)	. . . thought about how others felt:	

Learning Log (Upper KS2–KS3
(for the processing of lesson content)

Name: _____ Date: _____

Write a few words to show when you . . .

Disposition	*Item*	*Example*
(logical and analytical thinking)	. . . worked something out logically:	
(creative thinking)	. . . thought of something in a new way:	
(curiosity and wonder)	. . . asked a 'What if . . . ?' question:	
(prediction and inference)	. . . thought of what might happen next:	

Disposition	Item	Example (words or picture)
(resilience)	. . . battled on when you were stuck:	
(motivation)	. . . worked hard and persevered in order to do something really well:	
(honesty)	. . . admitted when you got something wrong:	
(community/ethics)	. . . did what you thought was right, just and true:	
(applying prior knowledge and experience)	. . . used a skill or piece of information you already knew:	

Disposition	Item	Example (words or picture)
(planning and organisation)	. . . planned and organised yourself or your group well:	
(independence)	. . . worked independently and showed personal initiative:	
(balance/decision-making)	. . . made a difficult decision based on all the available evidence:	
(collaboration)	. . . worked cooperatively with others:	
(empathy)	. . . thought about how others felt:	

Interest Audit
'Jamie Oliver's Apprentice'

You are invited to spend a week with someone famous in her (or his) field. This person will introduce you to her way of life, her friends and work colleagues, and her ways of working. All your expenses will be paid. Who would you choose to spend your week with? Availability isn't guaranteed, so choose three individuals from three *different* fields of achievement. State the field/s of achievement if this isn't obvious.

1st choice: _____

2nd choice: _____

3rd choice: _____

You are expected to provide an account of your experiences on your return to school. The audience will be other students and staff in your school. What form will this presentation or account take?
Place a tick against three formats only, and rank these from 1 to 3 (with '1' being your first choice):

Format	*Ranking*	*Format*	*Ranking*
A 10-minute speech	_____	A written report	_____
A PowerPoint presentation	_____	A mind-mapped diagram	_____
An exhibition of photographs	_____	A painting or poster	_____
An edited video-diary	_____	A song or tune	_____
A choreographed dance (in any style)	_____	A role-play	_____
A rhyming poem	_____	A taped interview	_____
Extracts from your diary	_____	A display of materials (catalogued and labelled)	_____

Some other format? (e.g. a meal for four, if you accompanied Jamie Oliver).

State what format, and ranking: _____ _____

Which of these formats are you *least* likely to choose? _____

Your name: _____   Date: _____

Questions for discussion

- Classrooms aren't children's museums. How realistic is it to aim for 'authentic assessment' in a modern primary or secondary school?

- Do we lose focus and clarity when we combine cognitive abilities with emotional or social considerations?

- Is an interest in something related to an aptitude for something?

3.4 Identification through provision: the role of parents

> The ideal home would naturally have a workshop where the child could work out his constructive instincts. It would have a miniature laboratory in which his enquiries could be directed. The life of the child would extend out of doors to the garden, surrounding fields, and forests. He would have his excursions, his walks and talks, in which the larger world out of doors would open to him. Now, if we organise and generalise all of this, we have the ideal school.
>
> (John Dewey, *The School and Society*)

It's an obvious truism – true in most instances – that no-one (other than the child herself) knows a child as well as her parents. And parents are usually in a strong position to offer teachers surprising insights into their child's secret dreams, passions and abilities. The newsletters of the National Association for Gifted Children (NAGC) provide many instances of cases in which what the school knows about a child reflects only a small part of what that child's parents know. Where the gap between home and school knowledge of a child is too large, the risk is that the child may experience too few opportunities to develop his gifts and talents to the full, especially if these are relatively narrow or specialised: deficits can be more conspicuous than gifts, and their identification and remediation far more damaging to the growing child's sense of self. The usual opportunities for home–school liaison – parents' evenings, pick-ups and drop-offs (for younger children) – can be very useful for sharing relevant information of this sort, but for a school wishing to create an audit of the gifts and talents lurking on its roll, some form of standard questionnaire could be useful. An example is provided of a questionnaire that seeks to elicit narrative feedback from a parent, and a questionnaire which attempts to profile a child's multiple intelligences:

Parents' Questionnaire:
Towards an audit of our students' gifts and talents

Name of child: _____ Date of completion: _____

Class: _____

What does your child do really well?

What single achievement do you think your child is proudest of?

What sort of people does your child most like to be with?

What do your friends most admire in your child?

What does your child most enjoy about school?

What aspect of schoolwork does your child most enjoy?

What does your child most like doing at home?

What seems most important to your child at this time in his or her life?

Is there anything else which might help us identify your child's particular gifts and talents?

| | Multiple Intelligences Profile of Your Child | | | | |

Please let us know how you see your child's strengths and weaknesses. Place a tick in the column that best suits your understanding of your child's abilities, preferences and interests. Feel free to change any items that you think need changing:

Item	Characteristic	Below average	Average	Above average	Exceptional
V 1	Reading for pleasure and information				
V 2	Spelling				
V 3	Creative writing (e.g. stories, poetry, plays)				
V 4	Vocabulary				
V 5	Expressing thoughts and ideas in speech				
V 6	Enjoying language-based jokes and word games				
V 7	Memory for names, labels, terms, phrases and sayings				
V 8	'Talking around' problems – using language to aid thinking and planning				
L 1	Finding patterns and relationships among objects and numbers				
L 2	Good at arithmetic problems				
L 3	Good at other areas of maths				
L 4	Logical, scientific approach to problems				
L 5	Attraction to games of strategy or logic				

Item	Characteristic	Below average	Average	Above average	Exceptional
L 6	Grasping connections/links between concepts				
L 7	Application of non-verbal reasoning to problems or situations				
L 8	Seeking of clear, reasoned solutions				
S 1	Model-making/constructional skills				
S 2	Map-reading/sense of direction				
S 3	Sensitivity to shape and colour				
S 4	Good at art and design				
S 5	Understands charts, diagrams and tables				
S 6	Repairing or assembly of objects				
S 7	Response to jigsaws, mazes and similar puzzles				
S 8	Understands how things fit together				
S 9	Ability to understand or see objects or scenes from different positions				
K 1	Enjoyment of practical, 'hands-on' abilities				
K 2	Response to movement, rhythm and dance				
K 3	Response to physical activities and sport				
K 4	Enjoyment of drama, mimicry				

Item	Characteristic	Below average	Average	Above average	Exceptional
K 5	Solving problems by active manipulation and movement				
K 6	Ability to perform complex physical movements				
M 1	Sensitivity to/appreciation of music				
M 2	Sense of rhythm and musical timing				
M 3	Recognition and understanding of musical forms and patterns				
M 4	Ability to create music (singing, instrumental performance)				
M 5	Memory for melodies and musical accompaniments (e.g. to TV adverts)				
M 6	Ability to reproduce a tone or sound				
Ie 1	Relating to other children				
Ie 2	Relating to adults				
Ie 3	Responding to the moods of others				
Ie 4	Collaborative and cooperative skills				
Ie 5	Understanding of group dynamics				
Ie 6	Group problem-solving skills				
Ie 7	Appreciation of human differences				
Ia 1	Understanding of own feelings and moods				
Ia 2	Association of different emotions with specific experiences				

Item	Characteristic	Below average	Average	Above average	Exceptional
Ia 3	Interest in personal motivations, beliefs and values				
Ia 4	Sense of personal direction in life				
Ia 5	Concentration				
N 1	Appreciation of nature, the outdoors				
N 2	Affinity with animals				
N 3	Recognition of patterns in nature – seasons, cycles, links and interrelationships				
G 1	Passion for learning				
G 2	Passion for school				
G 3	Intellectual curiosity				
G 4	Resilience (persisting with a problem despite encountering difficulties)				
G 5	Perceptiveness				
G 6	Fluency of ideas				
G 7	Creativity				
G 8	Flexibility/lateral thinking				
G 9	Intrinsic motivations				

Key: V 1-8:   verbal-linguistic items
L 1-8:   logical-mathematical items
S 1-9:   visual-spatial items
K 1-6:   bodily-kinaesthetic items
M 1-6:   musical items
Ie 1-7:   interpersonal items
Ia 1-5:   intrapersonal items
N 1-3:   naturalistic items
G1-9:   items often associated with giftedness and talent

Questions for discussion

- What systems for learning about a child's abilities and interests from his or her parents are already in place in your school? Which of these works best? Why?

- If a parent were to tell you that his daughter, aged nine and in your class, ran a small but thriving home business breeding and selling hamsters, what impact would this knowledge have on your provision for her in school?

4 On becoming wise

The 'trans-intellective' domain

4.1 Neither geeks nor monsters: gifts beyond measure

> Great men are not always wise.
>
> (Job 32:9)

> Many of those who hid Jews or other persecuted people during World War II lacked education or sophistication. In contrast, eight of the fourteen men who laid plans to implement the Final Solution held doctoral degrees from major European universities.
>
> (Howard Gardner, *Intelligence Reframed*)

It is our firm belief, and that of the teachers and young people with whom we work, that education must transcend the narrowly academic curriculum. Of course teachers and other educators have always believed this to be the case, but in the desire to meet the standards agenda it sometimes seems to have been forgotten. An inclusive approach to the identification and development of gifts and talents has, as previously explored, to embrace much more than those 'intellective' domains traditionally associated with giftedness. As indicated by Zorman (1998), 'It is not enough to measure specific abilities and talents. It is not even enough to measure the ability to learn when given mediation. Rather, one must also search for the non-intellective components that may aid or deter development of talent and abilities' (Zorman 1998, quoted in Eyre and McClure 2001:9).

This chapter looks at how we might place the notion of educating in the social, emotional *and* cognitive domains at the core of what schools do. We undertake a search for Zorman's 'non-intellective' components, but given the broad reach of the mind and brain and the location there of our emotional, social *and* cognitive selves, we prefer to adopt the term 'trans-intellective'. Claxton (1999) observes that 'the idea of intelligence as pre-eminently conscious, rational and articulate is undermined by evidence of the vital importance of the other, non-intellectual compartments of the learning toolkit, and by demonstrations that hard thinking isn't very relevant to many of the smart things that real people do' (Claxton 1999:226). But why should a school working specifically on its gifted and talented policy be equally focused on promoting social and emotional skills and abilities? Consider these two stereotypes:

Case Studies

Martyn was a very able student with exceptional strengths in science and maths. He didn't have a happy time at school. The teachers were OK but he didn't find it easy to make friends and his peers teased him. This meant that he spent much of his time in the library, working hard to assert his intellectual superiority over his tormentors. He left school for university with many academic laurels – and a hatred of his fellow man. At university, in his personal life and in his later business career he maintained a strong desire to win at any cost.

Colin was a very able student at primary school. He found his lessons easy and unchallenging. In the early days he worked hard and won favour from his teachers, but this didn't seem to go down too well with the other children in the class. He picked up on their sneers and soon learned to coast in his lessons. To keep himself amused, interested and part of the crowd he learned to bait his teachers without getting caught.

Are these stereotypes familiar? If they are, it's worth emphasising that both boys *are* stereotypes, and we should have regard for the research which since the days of Terman (1925) has helped to debunk popular stereotypes around giftedness. In recent times this would include Joan Freeman's longitudinal study of over 200 children and young people in the UK (Freeman 1979; 1991a; 2001). We know from Joan Freeman's work that Martyn and Colin are unlikely to exist *because of* their giftedness, and their personality characteristics may not even demonstrably be related to their high IQs. Very many highly able students (however defined) are passionately preoccupied with issues around social justice and morality, and lead balanced, well-adjusted lives. The Third Reich threw up both monsters and saints: Heydrich and Bonhoeffer, Mengele and Schindler. Nonetheless, if Martyn and Colin exist at all, we might do well to reflect on the journeys they took through the educational system, and try thereby to address the issues raised by these stereotypes of gifted and talented young people. It's our suspicion that these issues affect us all.

Self-reflection around the barriers to learning

What do you think are the barriers to effective learning?

Take a sheet of paper and fold it down the centre. Following a period of reflection, list on the left of the sheet any aspect of student behaviour or personal attributes that you feel are a barrier to effective learning in your classroom.

On the other half of the sheet write the alternative opposite and positive behaviour. For example, if you wrote 'laziness' on the left you might write 'hardworking' or 'well motivated' on the right.

You might like to tear your sheet in half and throw the left hand side away. These are the behaviours or attributes that are undesirable in the classroom.

It is our guess that what you have written on the right is a list of words to describe a range of social and emotional skills.

This type of reflection, carried out either individually or in a group, provides a powerful impetus for attending explicitly to the development of social competences and emotional resilience in students. It is not just a matter of maximising learning. In our view there are more compelling reasons to place these aspects of learning at the centre of our education system. They could be essential for the maintenance of society both within and outside school. If you feel so inclined, you might like to carry out the above exercise again (by yourself or with others) but this time listing those aspects of student behaviour that are of most concern generally in school or those that are indicative of mental health problems, drug dependency or criminality later in life.

Paying attention to emotional resilience and social competence in schools has many advantages. It focuses attention on student behaviour and student learning at the same time as it focuses on enhancing the social environment – and this in turn provides an environment where these skills can be promoted (Goleman 1996). This leads to a virtuous cycle and creates an environment where individual differences are nurtured and valued, and where aspiration and achievement in all areas are encouraged by staff and other students alike.

4.2 The art of being wise

> The defining characteristic of wisdom is the breadth of considerations taken into account when rendering a judgment or recommending a course of action.
>
> (Howard Gardner, *Intelligence Reframed*)

> It is not a mind, it is not a body that we erect,
> but it is a man, and we must not make two parts of him.
>
> (Montaigne, *Essays* I.xxv)

Social competence and emotional resilience are necessary but not sufficient for effective learning and be-ing to occur. Being able to think logically, analytically and creatively are also very important – as is being able to organise and act independently. Robert Sternberg gave us the model and the words to allow us to bring these all together when he delineated his balance theory of wisdom. This brings practical, interpersonal, intrapersonal and extrapersonal interests into the same model and provides us with an umbrella and a starting point to consider the core skills and abilities required to be an effective and humane person at school and in society. Mirroring Gardner (above) Sternberg notes, 'The ultimate test of whether a judgement is wise is in how the judgement is made, rather than in what the judgement is. Two individuals can come to different conclusions, but both be wise if they fulfil the criteria specified by the balance theory' (Sternberg 2000:254–5).

In the BCLP we have set ourselves the task of attempting to consider how we can first identify and then teach (and students learn) the prerequisite skills that are necessary if we are even to begin to aspire to be wise and to make wise judgements in our lives. It may sound overblown and unnecessary, but if you consider some of the simplest, most prosaic choices you make in life then the challenge starts to become more practical. First thing this morning, I made a choice about what to wear. Even this very workaday event requires the accommodation of a range of external and internal interests and intelligences: the interpersonal skill of empathy as I considered how my audience might receive me, the intrapersonal skill of how I might feel in front of the audience, the extrapersonal skill in understanding the message I might be giving about the organisation I was representing. All these needed to be balanced against the more practical skills of predicting the temperature both inside and outside my workplace. Are these wise skills? Consider the following scenario:

Reflection: What are wise skills? (A task for both adults and students)

Sam opened the door. Paul was waiting for him. They always went to school together. Sam was just about to set off when Kylie, his little sister, shouted to him. She had lost her favourite teddy. Sam thought he had seen it somewhere upstairs but he wasn't quite sure where. If he didn't hurry he would be late for school. He knew his sister wouldn't be able to find the teddy. He looked in the kitchen. Mum was really busy with the baby. She looked really tired. Sam started to leave but Kylie started to cry. She was going to work herself up into a real temper. Sam said, 'I've got to go back,' but Paul was tired of waiting. 'I'm going,' Paul said.

- Consider what Sam should have done.
- Now reflect upon and list the skills and abilities you drew upon to make your decision as wise as possible.

When we asked teachers and students to do a task similar to this one they come up with a range of skills and abilities that we decided to call Wise Skills and Dispositions. They can be summarised as follows:

Wise Skills and Dispositions

Thinking – e.g. logical and analytical thinking, planning and organisation, creative thinking

Making wise choices – e.g. keeping a balance, taking risks, decision-making, being honest

Reflection – e.g. empathy, using past experience and knowledge, curiosity and wonder, enquiry

Working, playing and living together – e.g. sociability, belonging to a community, teamwork, communication, empathy

Feeling good about ourselves – e.g. independence, self-esteem, emotional resilience and well-being, motivation

How do our own skills and abilities fit in with these? The last section of this chapter will look at how through reflection we might discover how to create a wise school that teaches, promotes and encourages students to learn these essential wise skills. The acquisition of skills provides us with the option to exercise choice. The acquisition of wise skills provides us with the option of exercising wise choices, drawing with discernment and careful judgement on all relevant factors. As noted by Robert Fisher in his description of the Socratic method in education, 'If I really and fully knew which course of action was best, how could I fail to follow it?' (Fisher 1998:41).

4.3 Placing wise skills at the heart of teaching and learning

> The intuitive mind is a sacred gift and the rational mind is a faithful servant.
> We have created a society that honours the servant and has forgotten the gift.
>   (attributed to Albert Einstein)

> Facts are like fish. They go off.
>   (attributed to Oscar Wilde)

If one is convinced as to the truth and logic of the need actively to promote wise skills, abilities and dispositions then the great challenge is to consider how this might be done. The wise skills and dispositions are the building blocks of being wise, but they are not the cement or the bricklayer. This section considers how these skills and dispositions might be promoted in school. Mirroring differing approaches to the development of thinking skills (cf. McGuinness 1999) it is tempting to opt for one of two broad mechanisms for transmission: do we go for an across-the-curriculum infusion model or for explicit teaching within a discrete lesson? While we believe that an infusion approach holds perhaps greatest potential, the only way to be effective is to place these skills and dispositions at the heart of what we do, in all areas of school life. One possible way of looking at this is as the triad of approaches in Figure 4.1.

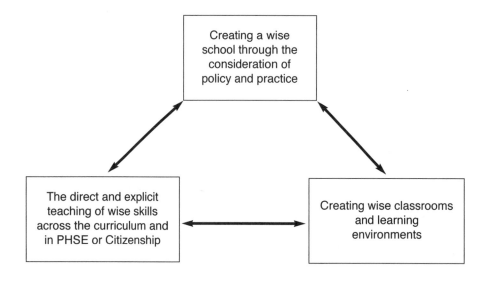

Figure 4.1   Triad of intervention

In relation to the wise skills listed in section 4.2, it is worth considering all the strategies that help students to learn these skills that may already be in place in any one school. It might be helpful for individual readers to return to the list of wise skills (see p. 53), to reread them and explicitly to list some of these strategies. When we consider these skills and dispositions it becomes clear that they are about our very 'be-ing' and that one of the most powerful vehicles for learning these is by simply living within an environment that operates with these wise skills at its core. However hard we might 'teach' them in an active sense, they will not be generalised and learned unless the social, emotional and physical environment is based upon wise principles. The need for genuineness and congruence between what we say and teach and what we do is at the core of our beliefs about working to develop wise thinking, wise learning and wise behaviour in our students in and out of school.

Creating wise schools

If we take Robert Sternberg's definition of wisdom as the starting point for our thinking, a wise school can be seen as being one that uses wise processes to make wise choices. Creating a wise school will be part of a reflective process in which the need to promote 'wise' skills and dispositions is seen as underpinning all decisions. All the school's policy and practice will in time come under scrutiny within the normal review cycle, but some decisions will be more important than others. Reflecting upon the wider impact of policy and practice will be important. Consider these two policy decisions at this (hypothetical) school and reflect upon whether or not they were wise:

Case Study

It was decided that the school would start at 8.00 in the morning and finish at 2.00 in the afternoon. The senior management team thought that money would be saved, as there would be no need for midday supervisors and kitchen staff. It was argued that students were more motivated and effective learners in the morning than in the afternoon and that the change would inevitably reduce behaviour difficulties and improve standards. Some staff argued that reducing opportunities for social interaction would be detrimental to the development of social skills and make it harder to build a school community. Others wondered whether students would be able to sustain concentration without a dinner break.

A new marking policy was to be written in a desire to improve student performance. Following a literature search about motivation it was agreed that staff would choose a limited number of pieces of work for detailed marking and that these would be marked in an informative style that was encouraging but provided clear guidance for future improvement. Students would be encouraged to value improvement relative to past performance.

In the above scenario, wise decisions would include those that involved

- further research;
- balancing the emotional, social and rational reasons behind the policy options;
- time for considered reflection.

Following the implementation of any decisions it would then be necessary to evaluate the impact of any change on all three key areas of student development (cognitive, social, emotional) and be willing to change if appropriate.

Creating wise schools is not easy and it takes considerable commitment on the part of all members of the school community. They work towards building a sense of community among students where they feel emotionally safe with their social and learning needs met. The adults in the school play an essential role, and considering their emotional well-being, self-esteem and motivation will be a crucial element of any work to create a wise school. It will be necessary to develop support systems for staff and create a social and emotional climate in the staff room where relationships are built on trust and respect.

Creating wise classrooms

It is hard to say what a wise classroom might look like. You would only know if something is wise by considering how it was created and how decisions were reached. A wise classroom, therefore, is one where all involved (staff and students) are provided with the opportunity to make balanced judgements and to exercise careful, discerning choices. And to do that there is a need for all members of the class to feel emotionally safe. This is only possible within a climate of mutual respect where the students feel there are fair boundaries that create social order. The class will be organised to allow opportunities to develop the wise skills and dispositions. This will require the chance to

- work in a variety of ways including collaboratively and autonomously;
- plan and organise work;
- learn the language of emotions and thinking;
- be creative;
- make choices about their learning.

Reflection: Good behaviour?

Elspeth, Paul and Maria are teachers. They are all described in their schools as being effective classroom practitioners. Their classes are well organised and there are very few incidents of misbehaviour. This is what they said about their approach to behaviour management in their classes:

Elspeth

I know I am effective in my classroom. Who wouldn't be after teaching for ten years? My success comes from good organisation and excellent control. I know what I expect from the pupils and it doesn't take long for my classes to fit in with the way I want them to behave. I have a few rules that I tell the class at the beginning of each year and then I blitz any misbehaviour for the first half-term. The pupils soon get the message that I don't tolerate any silly behaviour in my class.

Paul

To me, keeping an orderly classroom is all about balance and respect. I want the students to play an active role in the process. At the beginning of the year we work together to consider what sort of class environment we want and set our 'rights and responsibilities'. When I first did this I was a little worried that the students would like a free-for-all, but in my ten years of teaching I have always been surprised at the mature way they work together to establish the classroom climate. My job from then on is to act as a facilitator to ensure that our rights are not infringed and we carry out our responsibilities. Of course some children misbehave in my class but that is a way that they might learn about themselves and their behaviour. I don't think my approach is an easy option for anyone. I give students an opportunity to make choices about their behaviour and if they make a bad choice I will always follow up with an appropriate consequence. I have a class reward system in place that I can use for good social skills, good behaviour and for students who make a particular effort.

Maria

I see all the students in my class as individuals with their own problems and individual ways of working. It is my job to work hard to make sure these needs are being met. Out of the 30 children in my class 15 of them have particular problems. It is not possible for them all to be treated in the same way. I have had a few parents who have come in to see me complaining that their child feels bad because they are always good and they never get a reward, while the naughty children get more rewards. What they don't understand is the problems these children have. My biggest problem is the volume of work. I arrive at school at 7 a.m. every day and never leave until after 6 p.m. I have to be alert to avoid problems all day, and by the time I get home I am emotionally exhausted. My head teacher says I should find time for myself. I started going to the gym but soon stopped. I couldn't relax because I worried about all the work I had to do.

Which teacher do you think would make the greatest contribution to a wise school and why?

Creating wise learning opportunities

It is our belief not only that wise skills are caught by osmosis but that there is a body of skills, values and understandings that underpin them. It is important that these are planned in a systematic way into the curriculum. They might be seen as the skills and abilities that underpin Citizenship and PSHE, but they might actively be taught within tutorial sessions or planned across the curriculum. How do we ensure that we cover the full range of skills and abilities? In some BCLP primary schools staff have chosen to identify a 'wise' focus for each half-term, and then for each week a key learning outcome has been identified that is taught and promoted within the PSHE and across the curriculum. Others look to ways of incorporating wise skills and dispositions in their pedagogy. There are some pedagogical approaches that would seem to be more effective at promoting the wise skills than others. Examples of approaches which lend themselves well to 'wise work' would include:

- experiential group work
- circle-time
- philosophy for children
- critical skills.

Examples of these approaches in practice are explored in Chapter 5.

Summary

At the beginning of this chapter we introduced Martyn and Colin, two stereotypes of gifted students in or leaving our current education system. They represented examples of students rich in realised or unrealised potential, knowledge and academic skills, and poor in the skills and insights necessary to lead balanced, productive, affirming lives. In the face of emotional hurt, Martyn chose to split his feeling and his social self from his thinking self, and to devote his school career to the advancement of his mental skills alone. Colin sought to place his need for social credibility with his peer group before his need to learn and to achieve. His reluctance to subject himself to the ridicule or the isolation which can arise from achieving in a culture notoriously suspicious of achievement or intellectualism has echoes in the BCLP too: our baseline data include reference to the willingness of primary school pupils to have their friends know that they have done good work. In Year 1, 88 per cent of students liked it when friends saw their good work. By Year 3 this proportion had slipped to 78 per cent. By Year 6, we're down to 66 per cent. There's a clear challenge here. We believe that by successfully teaching, encouraging and promoting wise skills schools will be able to help prevent Martyn and Colin living up to their stereotypes. This is done in two ways: by creating a social and learning environment of mutual respect where individual differences and achievements are celebrated and valued, and by teaching Colin and Martyn (and their peers) wise skills and dispositions – so their social skills are learned, motivation is encouraged and self-esteem is nurtured.

5 Teaching for giftedness and talent

Examples of inclusive provision

5.1 What does an enriched learning environment look like?

> A person learns significantly only those things which he perceives as
> being involved in the maintenance of, or enhancement of, the structure of self.
> (Carl Rogers, *Perceiving, Behaving and Becoming*)

> The world of your truth can be my limitation;
> your wisdom my negation.
> Don't instruct me; let's walk together.
> Let my richness begin where yours ends.
> (from Umberto Maturana, 'The student's prayer')

Underlying an inclusive approach to gifted and talented education is the concept of an *enriched* learning environment. While the term means different things to different people, the notion of enrichment has been associated with inclusive educational practices since the 1930s, 'when Hollingworth and others decided that it was better to keep the able with their social age group rather than accelerate or segregate them' (Montgomery 1996:71, quoting Gowen and Demos 1964). Enrichment is 'the deliberate rounding out of the basic curriculum subjects with ideas and knowledge that enable a student to be aware of the wider context of a subject area' (Freeman 1998:44). While providing certain students with subject matter more usually given to older students (content acceleration) could conceivably be seen as one form of enrichment, within the BCLP we interpret the term as Freeman does – as providing something *qualitatively* different for the students.

Except in a few truly exceptional cases, we see little merit in rewarding gifted and talented students (in any domain) with early access to an ordinary curriculum – a curriculum all will have access to in the fullness of time. And even in these cases we would consider acceleration only as a secondary option, after genuinely high-quality enrichment experiences have been introduced and still found wanting. Gifted and talented students have, we believe, a right to something qualitatively special now. And so do their peers, just in case they're gifted and talented too but don't yet know it. The case for all students' entitlement to a high-quality education is well-argued by Ollerton (2001), among others, and the difficulties inherent in deciding which students might benefit from enrichment are raised in Chapter 3 and won't be recapitulated here. It may, however, be worth exploring at this point just what the research evidence says about what high-quality teaching for gifted and talented students looks like. Joan Freeman (1998:52) condenses this evidence as follows:

Task demand
- New knowledge is presented within the context of a conceptual framework, not as facts in isolation.
- The teacher stimulates thinking by taking a problem-posing as well as a problem-solving approach to issues and material.
- The teacher teaches for clear 'scientific' thinking skills to greater depth than normal.
- Abstract as well as basic concepts are emphasised.
- Materials are used which are high in quality, and reading levels demand complex, novel responses.

Use of language
- The intellectual demands of a lesson are recognised by the level, speed and quality of the verbal interactions that go on in it.
- The appropriate technical language is used, rather than a simplified version.
- Word-play is encouraged.
- Questioning is considered part of everyday learning, to stimulate thinking and creative problem-solving.

Communication
- Students explain out loud, comparing old and new learning and ideas with their peers.
- Research skills are taught, so that pupils can expand on ideas for themselves.

Encouragement to excellence
- Students get own-time rewards on demonstration of high achievement. This takes the form of individual projects in accordance with an agreed teacher–student contract.
- Goals are set to a high, perhaps professional standard.
- Mentors are appointed.
- Creative abilities are nurtured.
- Projects are completed and work is monitored.

In the next sections of this chapter, a number of teachers introduce and outline approaches which they personally have found to combine most if not all of the elements identified in Joan Freeman's evidence-based synthesis of high-quality teaching for gifted and talented students. Their experience is that these elements are features of high-quality, enriched teaching and learning experiences for all students, not just for the most able. Thus, the teaching and learning approaches outlined in this chapter have been found to be compatible with and supportive of an inclusive approach to gifted and talented education, and in particular to the definition of giftedness and talent developed within the BCLP. Moreover, these approaches are all, to a greater or lesser extent, concerned with developing students' trans-intellective capacities – the wise skills, qualities and dispositions explored in the previous chapter. We're confident that many other equally vibrant and worthy teaching and learning approaches are to be found being implemented in schools around the country, with similar results.

Questions for discussion

- What does acceleration offer that enrichment can't?

- What does enrichment offer that acceleration can't?

- What sort of provision do gifted and talented students need?

- What sort of provision do all students need?

5.2 Philosophy for/with children (P4C)

You cannot teach a man anything. You can only help him discover it within himself.

(Galileo)

Thinking inductively is inborn and lawful. This is revolutionary work, because schools have decided to teach in a way that is lawless, subverting inborn capacity.

(Hilda Taba)

Philosophical enquiry with children – a personal journey. By Roger Sutcliffe
(Roger was a secondary school teacher of English, Maths and Philosophy from 1980 to 1998; he is currently Chair of SAPERE and Vice-Chair of the Values Education Council.)

Case Study

I call this piece a personal journey. It is, at least, a snapshot from my own personal journey, but it also suggests how an introduction to the idea and practice of P4C (summarised as 'communities of philosophical enquiry') can mark a significant stage in the learning journey of any person – adult or child.

My own introduction was via the BBC documentary, 'Socrates for 6-year-olds', broadcast in October 1990. This hour-long film showed the process at work among American youngsters at junior, middle and secondary levels. What was most striking in each case was not so much the cognitive challenges taken up by the young people – questions such as whether it is only your brain that does your thinking, or whose 'voice' you are using when you think to yourself, or how much teenagers should share their thinking with their parents – rather, it was the manner in which they share their thinking with each other. It is that manner – what I tend now to call the spirit of enquiry – which I believe makes the process remarkable, if not unique, as an approach to teaching and learning.

It is not that teachers as a group fail to value enquiry. Because, by definition, almost all of us have succeeded educationally and have carried forward enquiries in our own subjects and areas of interest, we might indeed value enquiry *more* than most other groups of people. The snag is that we tend to assume that the subjects we have been interested in (and, it has to be admitted, have a vested interest in promoting) are the most important things for all other children to be taught.

Children, I venture to suggest, do not always see it that way, and may wisely suspect that there is more to education than simply what the teachers – and, increasingly, the curriculum designers – put their way. This sets up a conflict of interests, which sadly but prudently most children resolve by buying into the examination regime with all its supposed rewards. What makes this such a sad process is the extent to which it either destroys or distorts the wide curiosity displayed by very young children. It is only exceptional teachers who welcome and encourage questions from older children during 'lesson' time. Such questions, if taken seriously, would seriously disrupt the lesson plan, and (it is feared) reduce the potential for other students to learn what they need to know (for exams, that is). Thus is spontaneous questioning in the classroom destroyed, and thus is the young person's natural desire to question distorted into, for example, a wilful challenging of adult value systems, or a questionable fascination with TV or pop-star lifestyles.

So, what makes the community of enquiry approach to teaching and learning different? Too many things, perhaps, to convey adequately in a short piece, but here are a few of the most important emphases: (a) young people are given encouragement to ask questions based on their own interests; (b) they are given help to frame open questions designed to engage the interests of their peers; (c) the pursuit of the enquiry with their peers is facilitated/conducted in such a way as to deepen their thinking while broadening their perspective.

Achieving the last of these is the most challenging task for the teacher/facilitator, and I think I can say, after nearly ten years of taking up the challenge and of educating others to do so, that one never quite measures up to the task: there never has been a perfect discussion (pace Plato and Socrates!). That does not mean, however, that it is not worth taking up the challenge. On the contrary, the satisfaction, to teachers and youngsters, of taking part in a 'really good discussion' is beyond words. On such occasions, one's sense of personhood is truly enlarged, because there has been a meeting not only of minds, but of feelings and values as well.

Do such meetings happen very often? In my experience often enough to make it worth the challenge and difficulty of cultivating a spirit of enquiry within classrooms or classes that often are not conducive to such endeavour. Now is not the time to go into details of why they may not be conducive to the endeavour but, again, here are some salient points: (a) many classrooms do not lend themselves to the horseshoe arrangement needed for person-to-person communication; (b) many youngsters, especially as they grow older, become more passive learners – waiting for the teacher to make up the questions and develop the answers; (c) at the same time, many youngsters have internalised a notion that education, like life, is a competitive, individualistic pursuit – so rather than being ready to build on each other's examples, reasons and perspectives, they are all too ready to dismiss them without reflection.

It takes time, in short, to develop a classroom community of enquiry, where the proper virtues of thinking can be exercised – virtues (not merely 'skills') such as sincerity, openness, courage, reasonableness, patience, etc. By way of illustration, I felt I made good progress in these respects with a Year 8 class that I had the pleasure of teaching for part of the year 1992/3. This was an experimental top stream English class at Christ's Hospital School, where the aspiration was to challenge the students to take their thinking into areas, even dimensions, where they might not otherwise have strayed. I hope/believe that the following transcript of a part of a videoed enquiry illustrates not only some unusual skills for 12/13 year olds, but also some social and intellectual virtues. I have numbered and described some of the skills. Perhaps readers will ponder for themselves the virtues of the enquiry.

I should just explain that the question arose from a remark in a text that the class was studying. In the light of my own remarks in paragraphs 3 and 4 above, it seems particularly apposite that the enquiry focused on the concept of 'interesting'. One might be asking oneself the question whether the young people found the very concept interesting!

Transcript of part of a discussion by 12/13-year-olds, February 1993

Question chosen: What is the most interesting thing in the world?

MARK: Well, I don't think it's really possible to actually find what the most interesting thing in the world is because it's all a matter of personal preference, really – the individual, what they find interesting.

KATE: I think it's possible so long as you're only deciding for you personally, but if you're trying to work out for a group of people, I don't think it is.

EMMA: I agree with this thing about, you know, personal preference. I mean, but[1] if there was a group of people and they were all one religion, or they all did the same thing together, they could agree, say 20 or so people, could agree that this one thing was the most interesting thing.

FACILITATOR: Can we just take that back to Kate – and say if you go with that?

KATE: Well, I think they might be able to agree on maybe the most important[2] thing, but I don't know about the most interesting.

MATTHEW: I agree it's down to personal preference, but even then, does that make it the most interesting thing in the world? – even for you . . . I mean, you need a straight definition[3] of 'interesting'.

FACILITATOR: Okay, can anyone take on board that question straightaway? – It WAS a question . . . Nick, you want to come back?

NICK: I'll have a go. I think interesting is – the most interesting – is the thing which would draw your personal attention[4] the most . . . But . . . it's questionable[5].

FACILITATOR: Come back on that, Matthew, and then nominate someone, could you?

MATTHEW: Yeh, maybe, but would that then make what you found – the thing that attracts your attention to it most – the most interesting in the world? . . . because there's nobody that's seen everything or heard everything or done everything. So I mean, it – possibly – it would make it the most interesting thing in the world for them . . . unless you're talking about their own world[6], the world that they have knowledge of.

DAMIEN: I think, as he said, in your own world . . . I think it would be quite nice and I think it would probably help if we could, sort of, in a way define[7] 'world' – whether you're relating it to the whole world as in the earth, or whether you're relating it to the world of knowledge that that particular person has.

FACILITATOR: I see a nod there. Can we make an agreement about that? Does anyone have anything to say directly to that point? . . . We'll just take Matthew's point and then we'll see if we can reach an agreement, then.

MATTHEW: I think if you're talking about the most interesting thing in the world, you're talking about the thing that's actually in the book[8], and I think that means the most interesting thing in the world, as in the earth.

FACILITATOR: In the whole world . . . Does anyone disagree with that?

MATTHEW: I think that's what it's saying in the book . . .

[*3 contributions going off in another direction*]

EMMA: I just want to continue the thing about what kind of world it is . . . and they were talking about your personal world of knowledge; but what about your world in your mind[9]? . . . and if you go to work, you'll have, like, a different world and a different situation around you when you come back . . . and they're two different things.

DIANA: Yeh, I mean . . . I'd just like to say . . . because if I went up to my science teacher[10] and said, 'Sir, what do you think the most interesting thing in the world is?' he'd probably say, 'Science'. So it depends . . . it depends what your career is, or something . . . A vet would probably say animals and their bodies and the way they think and everything.

ANNIE: Surely your own world is the whole world to you, and you don't have any knowledge past your own world[11], but that is your whole world, to you as a person.

DANIEL: Well, I think that in terms of what you like best, I think, you can reach a conclusion, because you can say, 'Oh, I like swimming the most, and that really interests me more than anything else,' but in terms of the whole world, I don't think you can.

TOM: I think that when you're saying about interesting, sometimes you could say something like a feeling you have, when you think it's really interesting and you want to find out about it, or you could say the most interesting thing is the thing that you want to do and that, sort of, like . . . makes you feel good, and you think it's interesting how it makes you feel good. It's sort of, like, two different ways[12]. Also, on the whole world, maybe in . . . when it says the most interesting thing in the world, it doesn't say your world, so you couldn't define it, because everybody has a different opinion, and it could also cause[13], you know, like fights . . . If you try to say, 'I think this is the best' . . . ' No, no, this is the best.'

MATTHEW: Emma said there's a different world at work, but, surely – or wherever you go – but surely it's your own . . . it's still your own personal world. I think if we use 'world' as like, I don't know, a collective noun, and ev . . . all your experience (your philosophy) – that might be a good word – I don't think it's a different world at all at work[14]. I mean, you could still say, 'Oh well, that's the way that the machinery works at work – it's more interesting than the way I make toast in the morning.' I still think it would be your whole world.

NICK: I'd just like to refer back to, sort of, the mediaeval ages when there were many hundreds of small villages around the country, and the villagers, they knew nothing apart, or very little, apart from the village life, sweeping, cleaning up and looking after Granny. They wouldn't have a vague knowledge of foreign lands or animals unless it's brought with a messenger.

NICK: Going back to what Emma said earlier, she said that people don't agree on what they think is the most interesting thing, but if, say like, you get loads, like a whole cricket team, yeh, and they think, like, oh yes, this is really interesting, I'm really enjoying this, this is really important to me, they could agree that cricket is the most important thing in the world to them.

[couple of other contributions in another direction]

KATE: I think you can maybe define more important and more interesting, but I don't think you can get most important or most interesting.

END

Skills displayed

1. Disagreeing, with example

2. Drawing of distinction (between 'interest' and 'importance')

3. Seeing need for definition, of 'interesting'

4. Non-circular definition, the introduction of interesting (!) new concept into definition, i.e. 'attention'

5. Reflection/meta-cognition, i.e. ability to stand back from one's own thinking

6. Drawing of distinction or, more precisely, disambiguation (two senses of the word 'world')

7. New call for definition, of 'world'

8. Attempt to establish common reference, and therefore meaning, of 'world'

9. Drawing of distinction (between worlds of knowledge and imagination)

10. Use of example

11. Profound questioning of supposed gap between objective and subjective 'knowledge'!

12. Another (very subtle) distinction, between what we feel to be interesting and what we show ourselves to be interested in

13. Projection of possible consequences

14. Use of example

Philosophy for children in the Key Stage 2 classroom. By Jenny Smith
(Jenny is in her second year of teaching. She currently teaches a Year 4 class at Abbotsmead Junior School in Barrow-in-Furness.)

Case Study

I began class philosophy sessions after completing a Sapere Level 1 course in June 2001. At the time I had an unsettled Year 4 class which had no real sense of learning together or from each other, including several children with behaviour difficulties. Although we only had the opportunity to have a small number of enquiries in the last half-term of the year, I was extremely surprised by the extent of reflection and thought I saw from certain individuals, and by the effect the sessions seemed to have on the whole class; the children seemed calmer, worked together and listened to each other more than they had in the past.

Since September I have held weekly philosophical enquiries with my class and have been able to see them progress dramatically. They are now able to analyse and verbalise their own opinions, and have the confidence to share these with each other in the open arena of the enquiry. They are able to ask and reflect on questions of real depth; asking and discussing, for example, 'How do babies learn?', 'What does it mean to be happy?', 'Why does he get angry?', 'What does "wise" mean?' They are developing their own thoughts and deepening their understanding of abstract concepts. More importantly I feel that they are reflecting more on a personal level, both in the enquiry itself and when transferring their new skills into different contexts; they reflect on behaviour in the playground and find it easier to ask questions in other subjects, particularly literacy and science. They listen to and learn from each other, acknowledging that I am not the font of all knowledge!

Philosophy is a lesson that all the children love. When the bell goes, the enquiry carries on, and when I can eventually close it I am surrounded by a large group of children all eager to tell me what they think about what has just been discussed. It provides the opportunity for those who have been labelled as having 'learning difficulties' to develop their thinking and communication skills in the safe, non-threatening environment of the 'community', while it allows the more able really to reflect on, analyse and develop their thoughts and understanding.

5.3 Critical skills

I am nothing if not critical.

(Shakespeare, *Othello* II.i.)

I am bound by my own definition of criticism: a disinterested endeavour
to learn and propagate the best that is known and thought in the world.

(Matthew Arnold, *Essays in Criticism* I)

Lost or found? By Rick Lee
(Rick is an experienced teacher of drama, former advisory teacher and currently a
Raising Achievement Coordinator with the BCLP.)

Case Study

The terms 'gifted' and 'talented' have always been a problem for me as a teacher. On
the one hand I accept that some people appear to be gifted or talented and that their
gifts or talents should be acknowledged and honoured. On the other hand I believe
and promote Rollo May's concept of 'creative struggle' – that a gift should be
regarded as something that needs nurturing and developing. What I seem to be
struggling with here are two issues which concern me regarding any discussion
about gifts and talents. First, there is the whole matter of how do we know what definitions to use and what criteria to employ in order to identify gifted and talented
individuals? This is further complicated by the idea promoted in this book that we are
all capable of demonstrating some evidence of gifted or talented behaviour – relative
to ourselves – albeit in some cases off the beaten track of the National Curriculum or
the traditional academic pathways. However gifts and talents are identified, the
second issue is simply to ask what we can do about them. What approaches, strategies or challenges can we – indeed must we – facilitate for these individuals?

One project which has had a significant impact on many teachers in the BCLP is
Critical Skills, an approach that deals rigorously with the questions 'How good is it?'
and 'How do we know?' Critical Skills is an holistic approach to teaching and learning
developed in New York State by a group of teachers with Outdoor Pursuits backgrounds. It is now called Education By Design (EBD). Their work has been promoted
in the UK by Network Education Press and has been enthusiastically piloted in
Barrow, Bradford, Bristol, Great Yarmouth and Central Scotland. It is a collaborative,
problem-solving approach which sets participants 'Challenges' to solve which can be
academic (content curriculum-driven), scenario or real-life (engagement with adults
beyond the peer group). These 'Challenges' have rule, form and content criteria,
which constantly provide the framework in which participants can creatively provide
their own solutions. This approach also constantly addresses the development of
skills and dispositions and demands that teachers facilitate in a warm, yet demand-

ing, negotiated, informal and exploratory manner. Of particular interest is the assessment procedure which has been developed and which is called 'Rubrics'. This is essentially a matrix of categories and indicators, which in some form or another many UK teachers will be familiar with. What this matrix seeks to do, however, is to indicate levels of expertise and competence – which can be both generic and subject – or even problem-specific. I have included below my latest draft attempt to show generic developmental stages as a 'Rubrics' matrix. The Categories in the left hand column are taken from EBD levels of expertise as applied to teachers and trainers, but are also useful as general categories for the assessment of performance:

Critical skills 'rubrics' matrix

Category	*Awareness*	*Action*	*Achievement*
NOVICE	Have a willingness to learn	Have a go	Get it sometimes without realising why
APPRENTICE	Recognise that there is some pattern and/or purpose	Repeatedly test and trial to gain understanding – often includes the Eureka! moment	Can do it regularly, if mechanically, but with occasional mistakes – often caused by over-confidence
PRACTITIONER	Learn from mistakes to improve practice	Can do it con-sistently with understanding	Can do it con-fidently with some flair and variety
EXPERT *(Is this where we start to recognise some-one as gifted and talented?)*	Recognise the level of expertise and feel confident about it	Realise the value of practice to ensure mastery of form and content	Show virtuosity by demonstrating complete command of form and content
LEADER	Recognise the responsibility to share knowledge and expertise	Inspire others through a com-mitted, yet sensitive, sharing of the command of form and content	Apparently without effort, live through an inspirational, yet inclusive, demon-stration of form and content – a guru

[NB this is my personal response and not the Education By Design official position.]

What interests me about this matrix is that it seems to offer a set of criteria which could be used both as an identification procedure and also as a formative assessment tool. It also provides a way of thinking about gifted and talented abilities and behaviour:

- It is possible using these indicators to think of someone who can do or understand something really well without having a conscious sense of that ability, as opposed to someone who can do something with virtuosity and with full awareness of his or her capability.

- It does not preclude quantitative or examinable measurement.

- It promotes the importance of a command of both form and content as an aspirational target.

- It promotes the importance of the need for an appropriate disposition to increase and enhance learning opportunities.

- It allows for the principle that we can shift our levels of:
  - knowledge of subject matter
  - skill competency
  - temporary or sustained disposition
  - all of these over time or place.

- It recognises that we can be at different levels for different things.

- It allows us to jump from one part of the matrix to another.

- It is a negotiated assessment although it acknowledges external measures.

- It embraces the principle of lifelong learning.

- It can be put into simple or complex language or even symbolic terms for ease of understanding.

Most importantly, I think it makes us think of 'gifted and talented' behaviour and achievement as positions on a fluid continuum and as such questions the whole idea of putting an arbitrary line beneath a snapshot selection process, however carefully it is managed. It enables teachers to create a multitude of opportunities and challenges for people of all abilities and dispositions. It also assumes that the highest levels of achievement are identified as leadership qualities – which is seen as being beyond virtuosity – what might be called the 'beyond the prima donna' attitude. An interesting exercise might therefore be to test some universally acknowledged high achievers against this matrix. Where would Mozart or Van Gogh fit and what does that tell us about our attitude to them?

Finally I will turn to what might become the 'lost' element in this debate. We are very interested to 'find' and recognise gifts and talents and to 'find' strategies to encourage and challenge those we have 'found'. Whatever means we adopt to 'find' these young people or even find these gifts in everyone, I must express one big fear. As a GCSE drama examiner I can spot an A* performance. I can recognise the moment of virtuosity. I shiver at the sheer audacity of such an example of sophisticated talent. I can give it an appropriate arbitrary mark out of 40. I then leave the room. It has to be like this to be fair – to give the examination dignity and validity. I appreciate that. However, too often in education, and in other parts of our busy lives, the moments of awe – those humbling moments that transcend the functional purpose of the exercise – are assessed and 'lost' to a scrupulously measured death. We must ensure that particularly when we are working with people with gifts – everyone – these qualities and experiences are cherished. Robert's secret colours of winter leaves need to be treasured not just measured.

When asked what he thought of his own work, Samuel Beckett replied that he had hoped that he had made 'a stain on the silence'. Some of us might be more capable of this than others, but we should all be given the opportunity. I believe approaches such as Critical Skills can create these opportunities and that any curriculum which is only content and knowledge or skills driven should be seen to be a narrow vision, particularly for those of us who are struggling to express or to find our gifts and talents.

The critical thinkers – inclusion through a collaborative, problem-solving approach to learning. By Mike Sheridan
(Mike is in his fourth year of teaching. He currently teaches a Year 5 class at Abbotsmead Junior School in Barrow-in-Furness.)

Case Study

I started using the critical skills programme in my classroom last year and have developed this learning tool through my own reflection and through further training. The following account of a critical skills activity tries to deal with some of the issues relating to inclusion that arise through this approach.

The lesson starts with the children being presented with the challenge. This challenge is designed to explore issues surrounding urban transport and, in particular, alternatives to our over-reliance on cars. The task, to design a questionnaire, is set within the following scenario: the local council are considering closing the high street to traffic and would like to find out what shoppers and traders think of the idea. The children work in groups of three or four. The groups have been designed, for this activity, each to reflect a range of abilities and skills.

As well as the challenge, the children were presented with a fact file on alternative transport systems. One or two children within the group became the experts on this and advised and informed the rest of the group. The challenge made explicit the learning objective and the children are aware of 'critical skills' which are being observed and assessed. This time it's working together and decision-making. They are also aware of the 'product criteria' – the expectation for the finished product.

When the challenge has been read and discussed in the groups, the class come back together and split the challenge into steps and things to be done. Once all are clear about the 'what', the 'how well' factor is introduced. This is in the form of an assessment rubric. An assessment rubric presents the criteria for success and what varying degrees of success would look like. Giving the children this information at the start of the activity gives them the advantage of being able to make decisions about how they might make their product meet such criteria. After the activity is over, children present to their peers and receive feedback from them. They then go on to place their work on the assessment rubric. This is the end of the learning activity, and the next stage is where the children have the opportunity to demonstrate, individually, the depth of their learning during the activity. This provides an opportunity for the children to focus their knowledge and for the teacher to assess individual understanding. This takes place a few days later and the children are asked to write an essay or mindmap comparing different forms of transport, including the pros and cons.

This problem-solving approach to learning is appropriate for the full spectrum of learners and it challenges and supports children at a number of levels. There has been significant evidence in my classroom that some children who would often be working within their comfort zone have found it very challenging working as part of an interdependent team. First, it has challenged their interpersonal skills. This initially surfaced as frustration at the lack of depth of understanding of other team members. However, once the children recognise this as part of the challenge, they start to develop their skills in bringing others up to speed with their thinking. My worry with this scenario was that their ideas would be instantly accepted. This was not the case. All members of the group developed an awareness of critical questioning and, through this, considered decisions are being made.

The second observation I have made is of the reflective thought demonstrated through the independent work that followed this activity. Because I have only recently started to make such a link in learning it is difficult to be conclusive about this finding. However, as a result of individual conversations I have had with children about their work, I am confident that this is a result of the process that takes place during the challenge. The real strength of this model is that it takes into account different learning styles. It is my firm belief that all children have strengths that deserve to be developed, and through this model children are able to learn through their strengths. Can all children be on the gifted and talented list? We all have talent for something at some level. Surely we deserve the opportunity to use it?

5.4 Other thinking for learning approaches

The Romans taught their children nothing that was to be learned sitting.

(Montaigne, *Essays* II.xxi)

I am neither especially clever nor especially gifted. I am only very, very curious.

(attributed to Albert Einstein)

Shaping up. By Simon Beswick

(Simon is a Key Stage 2 classteacher at St Mary's CE Primary School, Davyhulme.)

'When all you have is a hammer, everything you see begins to look like a nail' – Anon.

Case Study

Our school is exploring and driving towards the ideal of an inclusive gifted and talented learning environment – a journey that is proving to be both rewarding and frustrating in equal measure, as exciting opportunities arise and questions emerge that hold our teaching up to a revealing and critical light. A chance to reflect on this journey may well be opportune.

To start, I would like to share an analogy that I used in my first INSET, when explaining what I felt underpinned the whole argument for an inclusive curriculum: it was just over a year ago that I watched my then 18-month-old son playing with a toy that required him to fit shapes into a selection of given holes. The shapes that he had at his disposal were added to with wooden shapes that had previously lain unused at the bottom of his toy box. For a considerable period of time (probably only ten minutes) he concentrated on fitting these shapes into the variety of shaped holes on offer. Within his collection of shapes there were many that did not have a suitably shaped hole in which to be placed. This it seemed did not matter, for my usually so sensitive son had – a hammer! As I watched he proceeded either to fit a shape into its corresponding hole, or to force a shape with his hammer into an obviously ill-matched hole (but one that allowed for at least some entry into the box below), or to discard the shape unceremoniously over his shoulder.

As a Year 6 teacher I felt with growing horror that this was, albeit metaphorically, how I was dealing with my students. The 11+, preparation for SATs and an obvious weighting towards the linguistic and logical-mathematical intelligences replace the holes on offer. The shapes that fit are the children who excel, achieve, enjoy or cope with these intelligences. The shapes that didn't quite fit were the 'Booster' children, the 'nearly theres'. And the hammer? That was me, my words, and my actions as I strove to find a way for those children who did not quite fit, to fit. However, let us not forget those shapes that my young son discarded so decisively. Who were they?

It was with this metaphor in mind that I decided to create as many different opportunities for my students as possible and at the same time ensure that the children were aware of and a part of the whole learning process. My planning became paramount and I put together a staged learning process that allowed the children to see each step clearly. This planning began to take on a new relevance, and I would now suggest that it is a crucial piece of the puzzle that allows other elements to slot into place. For without a reason to work and something to aim for, motivation is easily lost.

There are, of course, many pieces in this educational form-board: thinking skills, gifted and talented, broad and balanced curriculum, emotional intelligence, national curriculum, citizenship . . . It is important to realise that an inclusive learning environment is one that embraces all of these areas and disciplines. Seen and used in isolation each of these areas will lose its power and become yesterday's initiative. Bolt-on activities they are not. For the whole edifice to fit and remain stable, each piece must connect to create a flexible foundation for learning. As an example, take Gail, a girl I have taught now for three of her four years in Key Stage 2. In Year 1 and Year 2 Gail missed a full year of schooling through cancer. Back in school through Years 3 and 4, it was clear that the lost year had affected in particular her language capacity. This then manifested itself as a lack of self-esteem, with acknowledgement on her part that she couldn't write. Hindered by extremely poor spelling and ill-formed handwriting she fell into ways of running shy of writing activities; concocting a culture of excuses to keep all those concerned for her at bay. Her mum, over three years of growing frustration, was convinced that Gail was intellectually limited and, in her own words, 'would never achieve much academically'. Gail offered me, as her teacher, a real challenge, for she was undeniably intelligent – particularly in oral situations, and certainly with her adeptness at evading work.

So what has changed? Let me tell you about a science topic that we have recently completed. The content was micro-organisms, with more than a doff of the cap to Year 6 revision. After a lesson to consolidate understanding, the children were given the task of researching, planning and producing a presentation for a class of Year 4 children. The presentation was to be no longer than four minutes, it was to be produced in small groups and contain a gimmick that would not only hold the children's attention but also enable some clear learning to take place. The children used a graphic organiser at the planning stage and used the computer both for research and to give their presentation a professional feel. Enthusiasm drove the children to work in dinnertimes and at home. The presentations were filmed for evaluation purposes and the Year 4s filled in a pro forma so that we could analyse our performances for improvement possibilities. It was within these pro formas that the Year 4 children paid testament to Gail's skills. Her group produced a play as part of their presentation and she shone. With great humour and control, she gripped her audience.

The question could be asked, that although this work was undoubtedly beneficial for Gail and most if not all of the children, does it act as a strong argument for an effective and inclusive curriculum? Indeed, there were others who excelled in the task, but for Gail I feel that this was the key to unlock her potential, by acting as an injection to her academic confidence. It was as if she had suddenly discovered that she had a place in the school. From a regular pattern of absenteeism she has had a whole term of unbroken schooling. She is enthusiastic about her work and her mother thinks the transformation is miraculous. The most pleasing aspect of this example is that Gail now enjoys writing.

An honest appraisal of the science work would show that there were children (three boys) who needed to be coaxed towards a worthwhile outcome. For these children this approach may not have brought out their best. But that may be the point. A rich variety of tasks and opportunities casts a wide net, and creates many more and differently shaped holes for the shapes to find a home.

So to ensure that I cast as wide a net as possible, I follow a simple pattern: from the National Curriculum I acknowledge the content, using thinking tools such as de Bono's Thinking Hats, Thinker's Keys, Graphic Organisers, and Bloom's Taxonomy. I involve the children in the learning process from the start. Then to give them a motivation to learn how to learn, I indulge my creativity in the tasks, projects or products upon which they will hone their skills. So far we have produced television documentaries, radio programmes, multi-media artwork, and combined music and letters to create the emotions of frontline soldiers. In literacy we have stripped bare the process of writing, moving from a flood of ideas, to focusing in on a specific idea, then finally producing a piece of writing. Thinking through each part of the process has unearthed some quite startling results across the range of abilities. Unleashing their thinking and ideas in the early stages seems to remove hang-ups and confusion.

As a teacher and a leader of thinking skills within my school, I have seen and am currently seeing an awakening of teachers to the enjoyment of the job. The classrooms are losing their lethargy and the atmosphere is beginning to buzz. Yet I do not think any of this could have come about if I hadn't committed myself to the work required to change completely *my own* teaching and learning mindset. This way of working requires strong and innovative planning, enthusiasm and energy from the teacher, and bold school leadership that is clear in a vision for education that insists on opportunities for all.

Thinking skills in primary humanities. By Elaine Jackson
(Elaine is an experienced teacher and primary head teacher currently employed by Trafford Education Service as an adviser for school improvement in the primary sector.)

Case Study

I have been working with a group of teachers (all at different stages in their careers and having different amounts of experience) for nearly two years on thinking skills in primary humanities (history and geography). Initially, we focused on 'one off' lessons, but as a group, we felt that using 'one off' lessons alone, as good as they may be, was not going to embed 'thinking skills' into the whole curriculum. Thinking is not an 'add-on' but an integral element in the teaching and learning of all subjects, so it was felt a more fundamental look at the curriculum and planning for that curriculum was required.

The group feels that the crux of developing a thinking culture is the effective use of questioning and discussion, combined with the explicit teaching of thinking skills to all students. The use of 'wait and think!' and 'think – pair – share' strategies allow individual thinking time. It is important to provide teaching and learning activities that will empower students with the language, tools and strategies to engage in a wide range of analytical, critical and creative thinking tasks. Focus on empowering students with the skills to reason, to make informed judgements, critically to evaluate information and to think creatively is essential.

By developing thinking skills, students can focus on 'knowing how to learn' as well as 'knowing what to learn', i.e. learning how to learn. Effective teaching is not about covering the content but about uncovering the learning. 'What counts is not what children know today but what they can do with it tomorrow' (anon.).

As a group, we secured a TIPD grant (Teachers International Professional Development) from Central Bureau, and we were very privileged to be able to visit schools in Adelaide, many of whom followed a framework for the explicit teaching of thinking skills. The work carried out by Michael Pohl influenced much of the delivery of thinking skills in Adelaide.

Following our return from Adelaide, the group has focused on questioning and different frameworks for developing thinking skills, including De Bono's hats, Bloom's taxonomy of higher order thinking, Ryan's thinkers keys and Gardner's multiple intelligences. Different members of the group have focused on different age groups from Reception to Year 6. Also part of our group are colleagues working with secondary-aged students.

The group also reviewed the use of graphic organisers, ways for children to get their ideas, thoughts, research and learning on to paper. Examples of graphic organisers include simple webs, concept maps, Venn diagrams, consequence wheels, fishbone diagrams, flow charts, matrices and mindmaps.

Our current work involves taking QCA units in history and geography and planning 'thinking activities' through our selected 'thinking frameworks' in order to help teachers to have an understanding of the many different strategies and activities possible. Examples are shown in Figures 5.1–5.3, all based on QCA Geography Unit 10.

Hat	*Activities*
WHITE HAT *Information* **Facts. Questions.** What information do we have? What information do we need?	Use the Internet and reference books to create a data file on India. List the capital city, other major cities, rivers and mountains, surrounding seas and oceans. Describe what happens at one of India's religious festivals/celebrations. 'India is a land of many contrasts.' Make an alphabet book for a young child, illustrating the contrasts.
RED HAT *Feelings* **Emotions. Intuition. Hunches.** No need to justify the feelings. How do I feel about this now?	Look at the photograph of traffic in the streets of Calcutta/Bangalore. How would you feel riding along in a rickshaw? How do you feel about raising money to provide aid for people in India? How would you feel about wearing a sari every day for a week? Would people treat you differently? What activities would you not be able to do?
YELLOW HAT *Strengths* **Good points.** Why is this worth doing? How will it help us? Why can it be done? Why will it work?	How has farming changed over the years as a result of instruction, aid and help from Action Aid?
BLACK HAT *Weaknesses* **Bad points. Caution. Judgement. Assessment.** Will it work? What are the weaknesses? What is wrong with it?	What might cause the rice crop to fail? Why may over-reliance on one main crop be an issue?
GREEN HAT *Creativity* **New/Different ideas. Suggestions and proposals.** What are some possible ways to work this out? What are some other ways to work the problem out?	Create a collage to represent the different physical features found in India. Develop a dance based on the Monsoon and the River Ganges or write a poem and/or song to celebrate the coming of the Monsoon. Produce a menu for an Indian banquet for four people. Make a mild curry. Make a representation of the mountain environment and rice growing areas through collage.
BLUE HAT *Thinking about thinking* **Organisation of thinking.** What have we done so far? What do we do next?	What have we learned about India? Which different ways of learning did you find useful.

Figure 5.1   De Bono 'Thinking Hats' – Put on Your Thinking Hats! De Bono's definition of thinking: breadth, organisation, interaction, creativity, information and feeling and action.
Source: Elaine Jackson (Adviser, Trafford SIS) and Linda Pickwell (Head teacher, Partington PS, Trafford)

Remembering (Knowledge) Factual answers, recall and recognition	List the capital city, other major cities, rivers and mountains, surrounding seas and oceans. Use 'Map from Memory' strategy to learn the position of the physical and human features identified.
Understanding (Comprehension) Translating, interpreting, showing understanding	Describe in your own words (with diagrams) the seasons and the climate of India. Use 'Living Graph' strategy to review 'A year in the life of a rice farmer in India'.
Applying Using information gained in different familiar situations	Use 'Odd One Out' strategy to reinforce connections between human and physical features in India. What instructions would you give a person making chapatti or a diva lamp?
Analysing Break into parts to examine more closely	Compare and contrast life in a village in India with life in a city in India. Use 'Mystery' strategy (organising statements) to explain your answer to the question. Compare and contrast transport used in rural/urban India with transport used in rural/urban Britain.
Synthesis Combine information with new situations to create new products, ideas, etc.	Develop a dance based on the Monsoon and the River Ganges or write a poem and/or song to celebrate the coming of the Monsoon. Produce a menu for an Indian banquet for four people and/or make a mild curry. Make a representation of the mountain environment and rice growing areas through collage.
Evaluating Judge, use criteria, rank, substantiate	Evaluate the effectiveness of the aid agency work in empowering farmers to diversify and grow different food and cash crops. When the monsoon arrives, who is likely to appreciate the rain and water and who is likely to consider it a nuisance?

Figure 5.2   Bloom's taxonomy

Source: Elaine Jackson (Adviser, Trafford SIS) and Linda Pickwell (Head teacher, Partington PS, Trafford)

Intelligence	Activities
Verbal-linguistic	Write a poem about life in Chembakoli. Use reference books and the Internet to write a journalistic report about leisure pursuits in India or traffic congestion in Bangalore/Calcutta.
Logical-Mathematical	Use the 'Living Graph' strategy to explain the traffic congestion in Calcutta during one day. Create a consequence wheel about what happens if the Monsoon fails.
Visual-spatial	On a map of India, locate major cities, rivers, etc. Design a poster/cartoon strip to show what life in Chembakoli is like. Use the 'Predicting with Video' strategy: Watch a video on life in India and predict . . .
Bodily-kinaesthetic	Make a model of the village of Chembakoli. Create a dance to represent the coming of the Monsoon and the increasing flow of water in the rivers and the growth of new vegetation.
Musical	Listen to Indian music and identify the instruments used. Create and perform a simple tune or combination of sounds using available instruments, which are representational of Indian rhythms.
Interpersonal	Write a letter to a child living in rural India, explaining your lifestyle. Plan a welcome for an Indian visitor who is unable to communicate in a common language.
Intrapersonal	How would you feel about wearing a sari every day for a week? Would people treat you differently? What activities would you not be able to do?

Figure 5.3: Gardner's Multiple Intelligences Theory
Source: Elaine Jackson (Adviser, Trafford SIS) and Linda Pickwell (Head teacher, Partington PS, Trafford)

5.5 Listening schools

> One must be fond of people and trust them, if one is not to make a mess of life.
>
> (E. M. Forster, *Two Cheers for Democracy*)

> The most fluent talkers or most plausible reasoners are not always the justest thinkers.
>
> (William Hazlitt, *On Prejudice*)

The BCLP listening school programme. By Ann Kendrick
(Ann is an experienced teacher currently working as a Raising Achievement Coordinator with the BCLP.)

Case Study

Strategies for increasing the involvement of students in the life of the school can 'encourage a sense of mutual responsibility within the school from an early age, promote positive behaviour, increase self-esteem and confidence by debate and action, and develop the positive role students can play in creating a caring community' (*School Council Starter Pack Supplement*, School Councils UK, London).

The BCLP Listening School Programme is a series of related projects designed to enhance the use of key skills for students. These skills include cooperation and conflict resolution, critical thinking, negotiation, problem-solving, reasoned debate, informed decision-making and creativity. The Programme is also designed to increase the sense of involvement and ownership of young people in decisions affecting school life. The BCLP Listening School Programme incorporates class councils, school councils, a partnership-wide student forum and peer support services. The 'Listening School' sits within a wider programme area known as Personal Development and Support. At the time of writing, the project links with many of the local or national initiatives in schools such as teaching and learning, citizenship, circle-time, P4C, PSHE, Behaviour Curriculum, the National Healthy Schools Standard, School Sports Coordinator Programme and education for sustainable development. Schools opt for the projects which they identify as most appropriate for their own needs, given the priorities of their school development plans.

The Listening School Programme aims to support the enhancement of students' self-esteem, self-confidence and motivation as antecedents to their raised aspirations and achievements. Specifically:

- Class councils provide opportunities for all young people to participate and to contribute, and in so doing to perceive their actions having a positive impact upon their classroom community. Our experience is that this esteems the learner, building confidence through success and motivating through tangible, authentic results. (In a class council students can experiment with the different roles of councillors and gain an understanding of the processes and mechanisms of the school council.)

• School Councils provide similar opportunities at a wider school level but also begin to address the area of 'ability' (or this could to my mind be read as multiple intelligences). Here, democratically held elections, including manifesto speeches, give opportunities for students with good interpersonal and leadership skills to become elected. Where the whole school ethos and policies are conducive, less academically able students are supported to present their manifestos. Consequently, there are examples of students holding the office of school councillor whose literacy difficulties might ordinarily bar them from election by peers but whose ability to work for the common good of the school community is recognised – through the support of staff and peers.

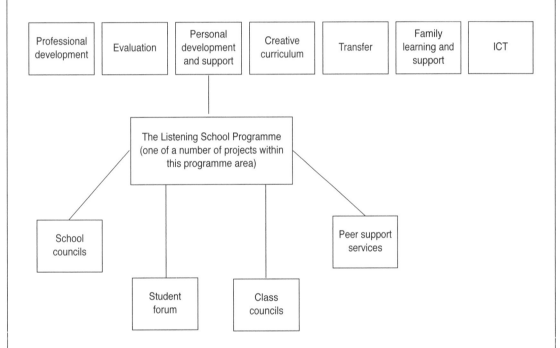

BCLP programmes showing detail of the Listening School Programme

Could it be that the election to and fulfilment of the office of school councillor provides for students to experience 'outrageous success as a learner', alongside warm, demanding adults, across a range of age groups, in a learning environment that supports exploratory, negotiated and informal learning opportunities (Christopher Ball's summary of the four conditions which seem most conducive to high achievement, as presented to a conference audience in 2000)? Such a question could also be asked of peer support services: is this an opportunity for peer supporters to develop their gifts and talents? Are peer support services also an opportunity for all students to feel they can impact upon elements within that community through recourse to their own resources, to support each other, learn, develop and participate?

The BCLP Student Forum is an informal, workshop-based gathering of school councillors and school council link teachers. Each school has four seats on the forum which are occupied by representatives from the school council. The Forum meets each term and the focus for the meetings is determined by the student body early in the school year. Over the past 18 months we have had five meetings. The focus for the majority of these has been the sharing and networking of one aspect of school council business, namely publicity. That is, how to publicise the role of the school council and through this to communicate and to involve the student body and staff within the school.

The BCLP Student Forum was initiated to serve three functions:

- to facilitate networking and the sharing of school councils practice;

- to give an opportunity for students to give an authentic presentation, to the student body, of their school's involvement in BCLP programmes or the work of the school council (authentic exhibition is a core element of the Critical Skills Programme, alongside the opportunity for students to solve real-life problems);

- to act as a consultative body through which the BCLP, community and statutory organisations could access student opinion, consult and share information.

When the BCLP was formed there were only five school councils operational. One had a history of ten years' standing while others were fledgling councils. At the present time, there are 11 out of a possible 12 councils operating and 10 out of the 12 have accessed the Student Forum. The Student Forum has, therefore, become a vehicle for developing a strong 'community of school council practitioners'. The forum is a venue for sharing existing ideas and developing emergent ideas and practice. The forum, therefore, provides students with the opportunity to see their school council as part of the wider 'community of school councils'. The relevance, importance and authenticity of their role is validated by the Student Forum and through feedback from its membership.

The Critical Skills approach (see Chapter 5.3) has been widely used within the Student Forum, because it is designed to develop a collaborative learning environment, using challenging tasks to enhance certain skills and dispositions while delivering curriculum content. This approach has an emphasis on formative assessment using a variety of feedback tools; these are being introduced over time to the Student Forum. The assessment criteria are developed as 'quality criteria', in collaboration with learners, prior to engagement in the task. An important strand of the philosophy of Critical Skills is the opportunity for students to give and receive feedback and formally to present their work.

The school council link teachers are seen as being an integral part of this community of practice. However, the teachers also form their own community with distinctive needs as facilitators of the school councils, each influenced by their own organisation's structure and differing attitudes to the concept of collegiality. There is also a developing community of Critical Skills practitioners, which interestingly includes the students, some of whom have been heard spontaneously to call for a 'quality audience' during their presentations!

According to Wenger (1998), who developed the idea of 'Communities of Practice', it is through such communities that learning takes place. For example, a school by definition is a 'community of learners'. In order for a 'fledgling' learner to participate fully in this 'practice of learning', Wenger identifies that the learner needs:

- access to active practitioners (i.e. teachers or other adults) within an authentic form of participation;

- opportunities to act as members of this community of practitioners and engage in the learning that membership entails;

- to access open forms of mutual engagement that can become an invitation to fuller participation in that community.

In simple terms this is saying that to become a learner the student needs to identify herself as learner – and to do this she must be given authentic opportunities to participate, initially at the periphery and then fully in the learning community. Thus, it is through the interactions of the members that communities of practice are formed, and through these interactions, established practices are passed on and new knowledge is developed collaboratively. Newcomers are, therefore, legitimate participants whose identities as learners are confirmed by the impact which they can have within the community. This is why school councils need to be a partnership between students and staff; not a battle ground for one body to enforce its will upon another: the Grange Hill Syndrome! Over time, school and class councils become a mechanism for allowing students to form an identity with the adult community of learners (the teachers), by giving access to a lived, authentic participation within the community.

In the student forum the process is repeated but this time some of the school councillors are newcomers and some are old-timers, sharing, networking, interacting and collaboratively developing new 'practices'. Moreover, particularly for schools, there are always newcomers to the office of school council, as year groups move on and new members are elected. This means that the opportunities afforded by the forum to accelerate the development of identity and practice become increasingly pertinent, as the clock is always against the link teachers. In collaboration with students and teaching colleagues I propose to continue the student forum as an opportunity for developing school council practice, and perhaps develop stronger links with the local youth forums. It may be interesting to invite local and county councillors to work alongside our 'gifted and talented' students as part of a student, experiential, enrichment programme in the 'wider community of councillor practice' – with the aim of developing student identities as successful high achievers in this domain.

School councils – one school's journey. By Sarah Ogden
(Sarah is in her seventh year of teaching. She is currently a Year 5 teacher at Abbotsmead Junior School, Barrow-in-Furness.)

Case Study

In October 2000 I was encouraged to set up a school council through a BCLP initiative. I felt that it was a way for children to have a view about their learning environment, i.e. the school. The BCLP ran various training sessions both for teachers and for students, encouraging the development of skills to facilitate the holding, running and minuting of meetings.

Each class in our two form entry junior school was asked to vote for two representatives to be the voice for the whole class. Children who were interested in standing for election were asked to write a short speech on their reasons for wanting to be chosen. The outcome and the number of volunteers from the class delighted me. All abilities and personalities were represented, which showed the feelings of self-worth that the children had in themselves. The children were asked to vote on who they thought would represent their own class in the best way possible. The outcome – various abilities, genders and personalities, gave a true reflection of the needs of the children across the whole school.

Our meetings are held regularly (fortnightly), and are well attended by the students. The children recognise the need for commitment even at the age of seven. The children also understand why their views are important, and that a wider audience will hear what they are saying. The children take their role seriously and always act upon requests for action.

As a link teacher on the council I have seen various children shine in the setting of a formal meeting. The children understand the need to listen to each other, without being reminded to. It is almost as though in this more formal session the children place a greater importance on hearing the views of others. Perhaps it is the subject matter. For an observer it is fascinating to see the children in this almost adult role.

I think that the most important lesson learned by myself is that we really need to *listen* to the thoughts and views of the children about their learning environment, especially when we are making decisions every day on events that will impact on their future lives.

6 Getting it together

Policy formulation and delivery

6.1 Components and connections

> Only connect.
>
> (E. M. Forster, Howard's End)

> 'Policy' (1): A course of action or administration recommended or adopted by a party.
> 'Policy' (2): A method of gambling by betting on numbers drawn in a lottery.
>
> (Omega Concise English Dictionary)

All schools in the twenty-first century are familiar with the requirements of policy-writing and some perhaps may even set to this task with great enthusiasm. Where enthusiasm wanes, it could be because the gap between the content and the delivery is seen to be too wide and the connections too weak, too artificial or too remote. Whether the theory relates to the practice might indeed seem to have more to do with lotteries than with 'courses of action'. For a school setting out to create and to implement an inclusive gifted and talented education policy, the connections *must* be strong if the policy is to be inclusive in anything other than name. It could be argued that the connections are inherently strengthened by the principle of inclusion, since there are fewer 'bolt-on' provisions to explain, to sustain and to justify. Where discrete enrichment opportunities do arise, these emerge organically from the 'default setting' of an enriched learning environment available to all.

Most good policy formats tell a coherent story, from rationale through to review and development. The format developed and promoted by Deborah Eyre at Oxford Brookes University has been used successfully by many schools for many years. It provides the framework for the descriptions outlined below and the example of an inclusive gifted and talented policy in section 6.2. The question-prompts will provide, I hope, a focus or point of reflection for schools aiming at an inclusive approach to this area of need.

Considerations for an inclusive gifted and talented education policy

Rationale
Why exactly do we need an inclusive policy?

- What is it for? (E.g. to provide a procedure for identifying and labelling? To meet pre-inspection demands? To show to current or prospective parents? To ensure accountability? Or to drive and to direct learning?)
- How does it relate to our wider school aims and philosophy?
- What forms of identification and provision for students do we currently use and offer? Are these consistent with an inclusive gifted and talented policy? If not, are we really prepared to jettison them?

Aims
What do we as a school community aim to provide for our students?

- Access to a suitably differentiated and challenging curriculum?
- Opportunities to identify and to develop their unique profiles of learning dispositions and strengths, gifts and talents?
- A broad and balanced education, including consideration of the whole person (social-emotional as well as intellectual needs)?
- A life-long commitment to learning?
- Good school-leaving grades?
- Flexible and adaptable thinking skills?
- An ability to work in a team, with people with widely differing strengths and weaknesses, skills and personalities?
- Opportunities to shine at something?

Definition
Who are we talking about? What constitutes giftedness and talent in our school? How widely do we (can we?) cast our net? Do we include:

- Only students with achievements or potential in the core academic subjects?
- Intelligences only? If so, whose definition of intelligence do we use? Are these intelligences illuminated by performances on pencil-and-paper tests, or by responses to real-life tasks?
- Students with 'trans-intellective' strengths – e.g. in empathy, resourcefulness, and resilience?
- A consideration of the context in which gifts and talents emerge? Is a child's failure to identify his or her gifts and talents our failure or the child's? What are the implications of this?

Identification strategies

How do we integrate our definition of giftedness and talent with the techniques we use to identify our cohort and the provision available to our students? Do we use:

- Checklists? Which checklists? Are they valid? What are their limitations?
- Teacher-nomination? Instinct and intuition? Structured observation? Inspection of classwork performance?
- Peer-nomination? Is this ethically sound? Under what circumstances? Is peer-nomination valid and reliable? How frequently is this reviewed and under what circumstances?
- Parental-nomination? How do we control for inhibition/modesty or for its opposite? How do we ask the right questions?
- Self-nomination? Does this involve deep self-reflection, or tickboxes? How do we create an ethos in which self-nomination might work? Who moderates, and how?
- Test results? Which tests? What results? Can we test for creativity and other qualities we might value? What is the test's 'ceiling'? Is the test valid? (Does it actually measure what it sets out to measure?) Is it reliable? (Will you get similar results each time it's administered?) Are test results compared with other data?
- Identification-through-provision? How do we ensure high-quality provision? How do we sustain it? How do we assess response to provision? How do we evaluate the data? How do we plan from and teach to the data?

Organisational responses

How do we arrange and timetable our class groupings for teaching and learning? What forms of structural differentiation do we have access to? For instance, have we considered (and what is our position in relation to):

- Forms of acceleration? To what extent can students engage in work normally given to older students? How is this organised? Within their own classes? In other classes for some of the time (e.g. for literacy or numeracy lessons only)? In other classes for all of the time (e.g. by advancing a student to an older year-group)? How do these options support or conflict with an inclusive policy?
- Forms of enrichment or extension involving withdrawal groups?
- Use of mentors and mentoring systems?
- Curriculum compacting enrichment groups?
- Cross-age interest groupings?

Pedagogic responses

What forms of within-class provision and differentiation to support and enhance learning do we make use of? For instance, have we considered (and what is our position in relation to):

- Interest clusters?
- The use of new technologies (e.g. whiteboards, mindmapping software)?
- Teaching for multiple intelligences?

- Curriculum compacting?
- Use of inductive teaching methods (e.g. Philosophy for Children, CASE)?
- Socratic questioning?
- Higher-order thinking challenges (e.g. activities at Bloom's (1956) levels of analysis, synthesis and evaluation, Critical Skills challenges)?
- Student-led research studies and individual or small-group investigations?
- Cross-curricular topics?
- Learning contracts?
- Differentiated homework challenges (cf. Goodhew 2001)?

Extra-curricular activities

To what extent do out-of-hours extra-curricular activities build on and develop opportunities for learning which exist as part of the schoolwide curriculum? Have we considered, for instance, the following factors and possibilities:

- The nature of the activities available and their relation to the usual curriculum?
- Capacity for uptake of an activity, and the transparency and fairness of procedures for limiting uptake where necessary (remembering that, in the words of a head teacher on the west coast of Cumbria, 'There is no wrath like the wrath of a British Nuclear Fuels scientist whose son is not included in a physics extension activity')?
- Class or year-group trips and residential visits?
- Lunchtime and after-school clubs?
- Summer schools?
- Links with adult societies (e.g. chess clubs, local history societies, etc.)?
- Creative frontstage or backstage involvement in such events as a school drama or musical production?
- Participation in school councils?

Social-emotional development

To what extent are decisions in relation to academic progress and achievement tempered by a consideration of the whole child? Have we considered, for instance, the impact on children's social-emotional development of:

- Their sense of personal involvement in decisions affecting their schooling – especially when these involve such pace and/or structural modifications as acceleration?
- Changes in friendship groups?
- Their need for peer acceptance and credibility?
- Their need for time to play, mess around and experiment?
- Their opportunities to develop such crucial 'trans-intellective' capacities as resilience, reflectiveness, resourcefulness, empathy, etc.?
- Their sense of 'ownership' of their learning – is it really their learning or ours?
- The quality of their relationships with staff and peers?

Coordination, monitoring and evaluation

- Who will coordinate the whole process?
- Who will supportively manage the coordinator?
- What is the timescale and process of plan–do–review?
- What structures are in place (or need to be in place) to ensure effective liaison and communication between staff, year-groups, departments, students, parents and governors?
- What opportunities for whole-staff inservice training are needed, and how might these be provided? A regular staff meeting slot? A training day or half day? Cross-phase or cluster liaison?
- How might promising curricular initiatives be evaluated for their 'inclusion factor' before they're taken on board?
- How are teaching and learning methods evaluated for their effectiveness and impact on inclusion, motivation, involvement, commitment, enjoyment, achievement, etc.? Are we prepared to countenance the use of 'number-free' assessment measures? Are we interested in the first instance in our students' learning orientation or in their performance orientation?
- Do we have the courage to resist the need for instant results, remembering the experience of CASE (where the impact on standards was profound and transcended curriculum boundaries – but not immediate)?
- Are we prepared to jettison our practices when the results are poor – even when these practices seem 'right'?
- Are we able to justify our practices to ourselves, to students, to parents, to governors, inspectors and other interested parties?

Questions for discussion

- What are the qualities likely to characterise an effective gifted and talented coordinator?
- Should the coordinator be a member of the senior management team?
- Is there a role for anecdotal evidence when reviewing the success of initiatives?

6.2 A gifted and talented policy for the Barrow Community Learning Partnership (Education Action Zone)

> Example isn't another way to teach. It's the only way to teach.
>
> (attributed to Albert Einstein)

Rationale

The vision statement for the Barrow Community Learning Partnership (BCLP) is as follows:

> The creation of a better future for the people of Barrow in which they will be able to extend their horizons and shape their own destinies through raised aspirations, higher levels of achievement, enterprise and greater self-reliance and independence.   (BCLP, *Year Two Action Plan,* 2001)

In order to help achieve this vision it is recognised that:

- the raising of educational achievement in all our schools is central
- effective partnership – at all levels – will help make a significant positive impact
- needs – at all levels – will require different responses
- resourcing will be linked to identified needs within the context of partnership targets and priorities.

Although there is no specific requirement for Education Action Zones to develop a gifted and talented policy, it was felt that the existence of one would assist with the prosecution of this vision. Similarly, while there is no requirement for BCLP schools to adopt a modified version of this specific policy, our schools aim towards maximum inclusion of educational opportunity for their students. It was felt that the existence and promotion of an inclusive BCLP policy would encourage moves towards the integration of planning for gifted and talented provision with broader curriculum development planning in individual schools.

The policy supports the social-constructivist and non-determinist ethos and values underpinning policy and practice within the BCLP.

Aims

The policy is intended to support the following aims:

- the raising of aspirations *for all students*
- high expectations of achievement *for all students*
- greater enterprise, self-reliance and independence *for all students.*

In order to help achieve these aims, we will work towards the achievement of the following objectives:

- for students to identify and to develop their unique profiles of learning dispositions and strengths, gifts and talents
- for students to be able to relate their learning provision and experiences to their personal educational goals
- for students to develop flexible cognitive, social and emotional skills and resources which will equip them for life-long learning challenges
- for students to have access to a rich, challenging and varied educational diet, which would include opportunities for sustained study of areas of significant personal interest
- for students to develop high levels of motivation and commitment to learning
- for students to excel in at least one area of achievement
- for students to attain the highest levels of achievement of which they are capable.

Definition

Within the Barrow Community Learning Partnership (BCLP) individual gifts and talents are seen in relative terms, rather than as abilities measured against set 'norms'. Factors giving rise to giftedness and talent are seen as complex and inextricably inter-related. These would include within-child factors (e.g. inherited or acquired predispositions, aptitudes and intelligences, learning dispositions) as well as situational factors (e.g. levels of opportunity, encouragement and learning challenge).

A gifted or talented student is regarded as one who has

(i) experienced a degree of facilitated self-reflection on his or her pattern of learning strengths and preferences; *and*

(ii) identified his or her area(s) of greatest strength(s) within the framework of an enriched learning environment.

Strengths would include gifts and talents as identified by the DfES Excellence in Cities initiative (G&T Strand) and also less easily measurable 'soft' skills and qualities such as interpersonal and intrapersonal skills and other elements crucial to thinking for learning (e.g. resilience, analysis, wise judgement and discernment, intuition and imagination).

Identification strategies

We advocate an identification strategy based on identification-through-provision. This is characterised by the following features:

- Seeing identification as process-based and continuous.
- Basing identification on multiple criteria, including provision for learning and outcome.
- Validating indicators for each course of action and provision.
- Presenting students' abilities as a profile rather than a single figure.
- Adopting increasingly sharp criteria at subsequent learning stages.

- Recognition that attitudes may be affected by outside influences such as culture and gender.
- Involving students in their own educational decision-making, especially in areas of their own interest.

(Freeman 1998:19)

Procedures and tools which support this approach will probe and illuminate from multiple angles, and these might include the use of

- self-reflection exercises
- evidence-based checklists (e.g. Freeman 1998:12–13)
- teacher-nomination based on a combination of structured observation, instinct and intuition, and inspection of classwork performance
- peer-nomination through games and affirmative activities (e.g. 'Mrs Fitzwilliam's Legacy', in this book)
- parental-nomination
- self-nomination through the process of self-reflection, communicated to teaching staff
- standardised and unstandardised test results, including National Curriculum tests, tests of attainment and aptitude available through commercial publishers, and tests of creativity.

Organisational responses

We encourage the use of a wide variety of class and students groupings in order to promote effective learning. This might include

- collaborative learning groupings
- groupings arising from curriculum compacting processes
- the use of mentors, including peer mentors
- cross-age interest groupings and clusters
- a degree of informed experimentation with groupings (with evaluation and review)
- where appropriate to the learning needs of the students, occasional opportunities for advanced enrichment work in withdrawal groups.

The general principles underpinning decisions in relation to organisational responses include an emphasis on maximising

- effective learning for all students (including self-knowledge and meta-cognitive awareness as well as the acquisition of facts and concepts)
- the delivery of an enriched curriculum to all students
- the active participation, engagement and inclusion of all students.

These principles are, we believe, incompatible with a policy of blanket student streaming, and even setting arrangements need careful consideration: where significant alterations to the usual inclusive mainstream arrangements are considered appropriate (and the general principles above are not violated), these alterations will be limited to the time, context and groupings needed for the learning objectives to be met or realised. An example of this might be the formation of an editorial board for the construction of a school magazine or prospectus, drawing on students with appropriate gifts and talents from across the school. Similarly, the option of pursuing forms of acceleration in particular content areas is retained, but it is expected that this will be appropriate for only a small minority of students, and only after

- the introduction and outcomes of sustained high-quality enrichment and extension activities have been critically evaluated
- full consideration has been given to the likely short, medium and longer-term impact of the acceleration on the whole child; this would include reference to the perspectives of the child and his or her parents.

Pedagogic responses

As with organisational responses, we encourage the use of a wide variety of teaching strategies in order to promote effective learning. Using an adaptation of the categories described by Kerry (2001), these would include strategies that are

- target-related
- task-related
- related to teaching and learning methods
- concerned with the pace of learning
- concerned with the depth of learning
- related to the resourcing of learning.

Specific examples are likely to cut across one or more of these categories, but within the BCLP they might include:

- teaching in interest clusters
- the use of new technologies (e.g. whiteboards, mindmapping software)
- teaching for a wide range of cognitive styles and learning strategies
- teaching for multiple intelligences
- teaching for the nurturing of learning resilience and resourcefulness
- teaching for wise thinking and behaviour
- curriculum compacting
- the use of inductive teaching methods (e.g. Philosophy for Children, CASE, the use of Socratic questioning techniques)
- setting higher-order thinking challenges (e.g. activities at Bloom's (1956) levels of analysis, synthesis and evaluation, Critical Skills challenges)
- student-led research studies and individual or small-group investigations
- cross-curricular topics
- the use of learning contracts
- differentiating homework challenges (cf. Goodhew 2001).

Extra-curricular activities

Within the BCLP it is expected that extra-curricular learning opportunities should build on and develop opportunities for learning that exist as part of the schoolwide curriculum. Opportunities exist for creative enrichment opportunities and links with the programme of Out of Hours Learning – which is supported by the New Opportunities Fund. It is expected that schools will ensure that procedures for accessing extra-curricular opportunities will be transparent and fair. Examples of extra-curricular activities include:

- class or year-group trips and residential visits
- breakfast, lunchtime and after-school clubs
- summer schools
- links with adult societies (e.g. chess clubs, local history societies, etc.)
- creative frontstage or backstage involvement in such events as a school drama or musical production
- participation in schools councils.

Social-emotional development

Social-emotional considerations are integral to our definition of giftedness and talent, and explicitly valued. Within the BCLP decisions in relation to academic progress and achievement should be tempered by a consideration of the whole child. Consideration should be given, therefore, to the impact on children's social-emotional development of:

- their sense of personal involvement in decisions affecting their schooling – especially when these involve such pace and/or structural modifications as acceleration in its many forms
- changes in friendship groups
- their need for peer acceptance and credibility
- their need for time to play, mess around and experiment
- their opportunities to develop such crucial 'trans-intellectual' capacities as resilience, reflectiveness, resourcefulness, empathy, etc.
- their sense of 'ownership' of their learning – is it really their learning or ours?
- the quality of their relationships with staff and peers.

Coordination, monitoring and evaluation

Within the BCLP policy coordination and monitoring of gifted and talented provision is undertaken through the BarroWise initiative, which is coordinated by Deborah Michel and Barry Hymer under the supervision of the BCLP Director, Mason Minnitt. Activities and projects which are relevant to gifted and talented provision will appear in many strands of the BCLP Action Plan document (i.e. in addition to those relating to Barro-Wise itself), but there should be a consistency of aims and principles between these activities and the BCLP's policy statement. Specifically in relation to the policy for gifted and talented, these activities should be appraised in relation to the following questions:

- Is the activity compatible with an inclusive model of education?
- What might the impact of this activity be on inclusion, motivation, involvement, commitment, resilience, resourcefulness, enjoyment and achievement? What measures are most appropriate to the evaluation of these qualities?
- Are benefits likely to be seen in the short, mid- or longer-term?
- Are we prepared to jettison these activities when the results are poor – even when these practices seem 'right' or in accordance with our ethos?
- Are we able to justify our practices to ourselves, to students, to parents, to governors, to BCLP partners, to inspectors and other interested parties?

Systems for monitoring and evaluating activities are as specified in the BCLP action plan. Central to these systems is the model known as the General Design for Improved Learning Outcomes (GDFILO), which provides a framework for assessing the relevance and worth of all current and proposed activity programmes, and for promoting shared dialogue about the creation of a professional learning culture.

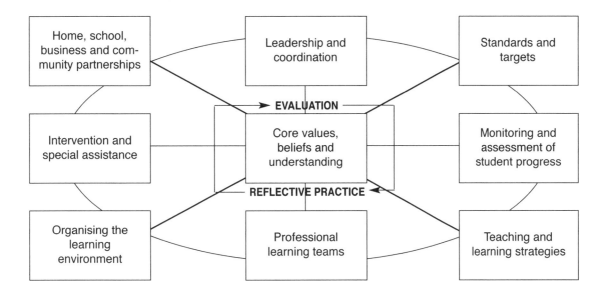

Figure 6.1 The General Design for Improved Learning Outcomes (GDFILO), adapted from a conceptual map published in Peter Hill and V. Jean Russell, 'Systemic Whole-School Reform of the Middle Years of Schooling', Centre for Applied Educational Research, University of Melbourne. www.sofweb.vic.edu.au/mys/pdf/phill.pdf

6.3 Last thoughts: policy and practice – a work in process

Alice:	Where I come from, people study what they are not good at in order to be able to do what they are good at.
Mad Hatter:	We only go around in circles in Wonderland; but we always end up where we started. Would you mind explaining yourself?
Alice:	Well, grown-ups tell us to find out what we did wrong, and never do it again.
Mad Hatter:	That's odd! It seems to me that in order to find out about something you have to study it. And when you study it, you should become better at it. Why should you want to become better at something and then never do it again?

(Lewis Carroll, *Alice in Wonderland*)

At the risk of seeming to spin off at this point into an alternative educational reality, it seems worth pursuing at least a few of the wider implications of a broad and inclusive approach to gifted and talented education. Some of these implications may seem paradoxical and to transcend the reach of any one teacher or school – especially in a culture of seemingly daily dictates and initiatives – but life and inclusion usually make most sense when they're seen as a conceptual whole.

Implication number one: There's little point in helping our students identify and nurture their unique gifts and talents if we aren't modelling these processes ourselves. Unless our students see us reflecting deeply on our own learning experiences, struggling to connect and make these experiences meaningful, and translating these meanings into new practices in the classroom and outside of it, we can have little cause to expect them to perform these processes for us. Because a focus upon learning can enhance performance (whereas a focus on performance can depress performance – Watkins 2001), we need to recognise the need for explicit talk about learning in the classroom. This resonates with everything we know to date about effective learning, as summarised by Carol McGuinness (1999) in her review and evaluation of approaches to developing students' thinking:

> the common features of successful cognitive methodologies can be characterised as powerful or high quality learning environments. These are: identifying high quality thinking as a classroom priority; developing a vocabulary for talking about thinking; making thought processes explicit through exploration, discussion, reflection and sharing; teacher modelling of thought processes followed by hints and feedback to students on their performance; co-operative and collaborative learning permitting students to become self-regulated; deliberate teaching for transfer.

(McGuinness 1999:29)

And the fruits of these rich learning playgrounds can't be for the students alone – we can taste them too, as long as we enter with our senses open to experience and reflection: Susan Hart has noted that 'Every teaching session yields a rich resource for teachers' thinking and learning, but that potential will remain untapped unless we analyse, reflect upon it and use it to gain a deeper understanding' (Hart 2000:7).

By extension, too, it would be entirely natural for a reflective school community as a whole to practise the processes described in this book. For a school to set out to identify its profile of 'gifts and talents', to make sense of the resultant data and to transform this 'self-knowledge' into something useful and actionable is perhaps not dissimilar to the developmental journey many schools embark on in their planning cycles. In this instance they would be mirroring at the systemic level the same cycle of experience, reflection and informed action that their students do at the level of the individual.

Implication number two: Perhaps paradoxically, there may be a tension between a truly inclusive gifted and talented policy and the popular concept of a broad and balanced education. In his book *Extraordinary Minds* Howard Gardner (1997) calls attention to a feature that is regularly associated with extraordinary accomplishment: what he terms *leveraging* – the capacity of individuals to ignore their weaknesses and to exploit their strengths in order to excel in their chosen domains. Effective leveraging derives from effective *reflection* (through which one comes to know one's profile of strengths and weaknesses), and should lead in turn to the third feature of extraordinary accomplishment – effective *framing* (the capacity to construe experiences in a positive and energising way).

Schools that choose to take on the challenge of developing and implementing a truly inclusive gifted and talented policy are well-placed, I would argue, to promote all three of the features Gardner associates with extraordinary achievements. Reflection can and should be an integral component of an inclusive definition of giftedness and talent. Leveraging becomes possible through this reflection, although it does raise the big question: do we really serve our children well by requiring them to experience a 'broad and balanced education'? Is it possible, now that Toffler's Age is well and truly with us (with the knowledge base doubling every 300 days), for any of us to do much more than scratch the surface of our content-laden and still-expanding curriculum domains? Arguably not. But maybe this is to confuse *education* with *curriculum* or *content knowledge*? Might our children be better served by giving them access to an education which is broad in the emotional, cognitive, moral and spiritual sense, but rather more restricted in the subject-knowledge sense? In this way, children might be guided towards a progressively deeper, richer, more passionate engagement with a more limited range of content areas, while simultaneously (and irrespective of the subject area) making connections with their whole lives – intellectual, emotional, social, and spiritual. But underpinning this leveraging journey *must* be sustained and deep reflection on individual experiences – before decisions affecting choice of domains for specialisation are made: to base any narrowing of options on such relatively superficial factors as prior attainment alone must be inadequate, especially in an educational system (and society) which is still based on a hierarchy of knowledge. Then follows finally the positive framing of these reflections and leveraging, which helps translate emergent understandings of 'self' into a deep self-knowledge – from which self-worth and personal achievements are more likely to flow.

Implication number three: We must learn how to value an infinitely wide range of gifts and talents, and the people and the domains in which these gifts and talents emerge. Again this isn't easy when we're still hung up as a society with Plato's academic legacy, in which some forms of knowledge, some disciplines and some ways of learning are considered superior to others. The notion of IQ fed and led this legacy in the twentieth century, but IQ's limitations were well known by the end of it. When the social commentator Ali G is able to ask of Rhodes Boyson, brilliantly, whether he feels 'thick' people should go to university because 'they need it more', we should realise that time's been called on academic excellence as embodying the *only* manifestation of intelligence, giftedness and talent. Guy Claxton (1999) charts acidly the historical consumption of education from the Middle Ages to the present day, noting that in his view the range of courses on offer in higher education has become broader and the demands less rigorous. This has happened, he believes, in order to encourage more young people to enter university and to receive the 'badge' not just of access but of entitlement. In Claxton's 'Academia Lite', the proliferation of degrees in 'Barbecue Studies' and the rise in the numbers of students achieving first class degrees tracks the steady cheapening of the academic badge. If this is indeed what is happening (and there are parallel debates every year when Key Stage 2 SATs, GCSE and A-level results are announced), it must reflect the residual power in our society of academic skills to represent the pinnacle of our intellectual hierarchy – and the reason why, despite the fact that they're likely to be earning around £70,000 per year after ten years in the trade (O'Hara 2002), plumbers are in short supply: 'The expansion of the universities is attracting youngsters who in previous decades may have opted for an apprenticeship instead' (ibid.:2).

As these words are written, there is in the UK a vigorous debate taking place around forms of assessment for more and for less able students. Level 6 'extension papers' for students in Key Stage 2 may be scrapped in favour of starred grades. GCSEs may be on the way out for 'bright' students. A few schools are having most of their students take some GCSEs in one year rather than two. The status, rigour and future of A levels is never out of the edu-gossip loop. Yet the skills and qualities these forms of assessment value and seek to measure are unlikely (however important they are in themselves) to be the sum total of our society's needs in the new millennium. In the twenty-first century we may well need accelerated learning, but we also need to be able to learn the things *worth* learning. We need both scientists to tell us how to do things and moral philosophers to ask why we should be doing them. We need geneticists to map our lives and we need people gifted in interpersonal skills and compassion to make our lives worth living. We need to think and we need to feel and we need to communicate our thoughts and feelings. We need more than ever to be connected – intrapersonally and interpersonally – and not just for the sake of our planet tomorrow but so that we can earn our crust today: we need to be employable at a time when our employers consistently and concertedly call in their workforce for the demonstration of such 'trans-intellective' skills as listed by Deborah Michel in Chapter 4 or such critical skills as outlined by Rick Lee in Chapter 5.3, or such virtues as listed by Roger Sutcliffe in Chapter 5.2.

Where and how are these learning dispositions going to be assessed and valued? Not, I would hope, by building instruments based on our past failures (psychometric measures of 'EQ' or Emotional Intelligence are a case in point), by trying to quantify the unquantifiable, or by devaluing the contributions of our plumbers or our gifted but juglexic tiger-tamers. We might stand a better chance of achieving authentic evaluation by working towards inclusion and towards rigorous self-evaluation; and, through an ongoing reflective loop, by getting better at it over time. In this way we'd have regard for the Mad Hatter's puzzlement: why indeed should we get better at something and then never do it again? Some schools have already started to explore the alternative possibilities of schooling for the twenty-first century (e.g. Hazlewood *et al.* 2002). For others, devising and implementing a truly inclusive policy for giftedness and talent may be a reasonable place to start.

Myself

I am the goddess
I am the Queen of the Stars
I weave and spin by the light of the moon.
I am the Gifted
I am the talented Creator.
I work my magic on everyone I meet.
I am the Golden Beauty within,
I am the experience without.
I know the knowing that is known.
I am the unique Princess.
I am the most special ever.
I have the individual power of succession and leadership.
I am the Ruler of Confidence.
I am the Empress of Shyness.
I have the wisdom and talent
And I will make it.
Yes I will.

(Holli Dillon, 13, Alderman Blaxhill School, written as part of classwork on the topic of human rights, and first published in the *Times Educational Supplement*. By permission.)

7 Support and further reading

7.1 Useful organisations and online contacts

The next best thing to knowing something is knowing where to find it.

(Samuel Johnson)

If you have any comments, queries or observations to make about the issues raised in this book, please let us know by email: Stillthinkinguk@aol.com

Listed below are details of a number of organisations which may be helpful in the process of working towards inclusive provision for gifted and talented students.

Bookstall Forum Ltd (books on teaching thinking skills and philosophy for children): email enq@bookstallforum.co.uk; website www.bookstallforum.co.uk

Brunel University Thinking Skills (Robert Fisher): www.teachingthinking.net or www.brunel.ac.uk/faculty/ed/Robert_Fisher/

CASE (Cognitive Acceleration through Science Education): www.case-network.org

Centre for the Advancement of Thinking (King's College London): www.kcl.ac.uk

CLEO (Cumbria and Lancashire Education Online – online educational resources including material for broadband, Foundation to Key Stage 4): www.cleo.net.uk

Critical Skills Programme, NEP Northern Office, 8 The Paddock, Gullane, East Lothian EH31 2BW. Tel. 01620 843506

Department for Education and Skills Excellence in Cities Initiative: www.standards.dfes.gov.uk/excellence/

Department for Education and Skills/Qualifications and Curriculum Authority generic and subject specific guidance: www.nc.uk.net/gt/

Education by Design (The Critical Skills Programme): Antioch New England Graduate School, 40 Avon Street, Keene, New Hampshire 03431, USA. Email edbydesign@antiochne.edu; website www.edbydesign.org

Gifted Resources Homepage: www.eskimo.com/~user/kids.html

Hoagies (miscellaneous gifted and talented resources): www.hoagiesgifted.org

Incentive Plus Educational Resources, PO Box 5220, Great Horwood, Milton Keynes MK17 0YN. Tel. 01908 526120; email orders@incentiveplus.co.uk; website www.Incentiveplus.co.uk

National Association for Able Children in Education (NACE), PO Box 242, Arnolds Way, Oxford OX2 9FR. Tel. 01865 861879; email info@nace.co.uk; website www.nace.co.uk

National Association for Gifted Children (NAGC), Suite 14, Challenge House, Sherwood Drive,

Bletchley, Milton Keynes MK3 6DP. Tel. 0870 770 3217; email amazingchildren@nagcbritain.org.uk; website www.nagcbritain.org.uk

Network Education Press Ltd, PO Box 635, Stafford ST17 1BF. Email enquiries@networkpress.co.uk; website www.networkpress.co.uk

Newswise resources: www.dialogueworks.co.uk

Nrich Online Maths Club: www.nrich.maths.org.uk

Office for Standards in Education (Ofsted): www.ofsted.gov.uk

Ohio Association for Gifted Children: www.oagc.com

Research Centre for Able Students (ReCAP) at Oxford Brookes University: www.brookes.ac.uk/schools/education/ablestudents

Richmond Able Students (for teachers, parents and children): www.richmondbrainstormers.co.uk

School Councils UK, 57 Etchingham Road, London N3 2EB. Tel. 020 8349 2459; www.schoolcouncils.org

Society for the Advancement of Philosophical Enquiry and Reflection in Education (Sapere): www.sapere.net

University of Connecticut Neag Centre for Gifted Education and Talent Development: www.gifted.uconn.edu

World Class Tests: www.worldclassarena.org

World Council for Gifted and Talented Children: www.WorldGifted.org

Xcalibre (cross-phase subject-specific resources): www.xcalibre.ac.uk

7.2   Recommended reading and teaching resources

I am enough of an artist to draw freely upon my imagination. Imagination is more important than knowledge. Knowledge is limited. Imagination encircles the world.

(attributed to Albert Einstein)

For ease of reference I have attempted to categorise the growing array of excellent books in the broad field of gifted and talented education. My taxonomical skills are imperfect: in some cases titles are listed in more than one section. While this is a fairly comprehensive list, it lays no claims to definitiveness and I'm sure many worthy titles have been inadvertently omitted. I'm also aware that a few titles listed are presently out of print, although they're often available in libraries and on school bookshelves – and good books have a habit of eventually resurfacing in the hands of new or different publishers. Some of the titles published in America are distributed in the UK by Incentive Plus (see Useful Contacts section).

For teachers looking for only one or two titles, I have marked with an asterisk those books which seem to me to offer an excellent general introduction to the field.

Assessment and identification

Black, P. and Wiliam, D. (1998) *Inside the Black Box – Raising Standards through Classroom Assessment*. London: King's College School of Education.

George, D. (1995) *Gifted Education: Identification and Provision*. London: David Fulton Publishers.

Griffin, N. S., Curtiss, J., McKenzie, J., Maxfield, L. and Crawford, M. (1995) 'Authentic assessment of able children using a regular classroom observation protocol', *Flying High* (former title for the NACE journal) (Spring 1995): 34–42.

Koshy, V. and Casey, R. (2000) *Special Abilities Scales: Observational Assessment for Identifying Able and High-Potential Students*. London: Hodder and Stoughton.

Lazear, D. (1994) *Multiple Intelligence Approaches to Assessment: Solving the Assessment Conundrum*. Tucson, Ariz.: Zephyr Press.

* Wallace, B. (2000) *Teaching the Very Able Child: Developing a Policy and Adopting Strategies for Provision*. London: NACE/David Fulton Publishers.

Creativity

Bowkett, S. (1997) *Imagine That . . . A Handbook of Creative Learning Activities for the Classroom*. Stafford: Network Educational Press.

Casey, R. and Koshy, V. (1995) *Bright Challenge: Learning Activities Specifically Designed for Able Children and the Enrichment of all 7–11 Year Olds*. Cheltenham: Stanley Thornes.

* Cropley, A. J. (1992) *More Ways Than One: Fostering Creativity*. Norwood, N.J.: Ablex.

Csikszentmihalyi, M. (1996) *Creativity*. New York: HarperCollins.

Forte, I. and Schurr, S. (1996) *180 Icebreakers to Strengthen Critical Thinking and Problem-Solving Skills*. Nashville, Tenn.: Incentive.

Hobday, A. and Ollier, K. (1998) *Creative Therapy: Activities with Children and Adolescents*. Leicester: British Psychological Society.

Maben, L. (1995) *Homework for Thinkers: A Year's Worth of Creative Assignments to Stimulate Critical Thinking*. Nashville, Tenn.: Incentive.

Marks-Tarlow, T. (1996) *Creativity Inside Out: Learning Through Multiple Intelligences*. Menlow Park, Calif.: Addison-Wesley.

Pofahl, J. (1996) *Creative and Critical Thinking* (activities). Grand Rapids, Mich.: T. S. Denison.

Sternberg, R. J. and Grigorenko, E. L. (2000) *Teaching for Successful Intelligence*. Arlington Heights, Ill.: Skylight.

General reading and resources

Clark, C. and Callow, R. (1998) *Educating Able Children: Resource Issues and Processes for Teachers*. London: NACE/David Fulton Publishers.

Claxton, G. (1999) *Wise Up: Learning to Live the Learning Life*. Stafford: Network Educational Press.

Evans, L. and Goodhew, G. (1997) *Providing for Able Children: Activities for Staff in Primary and Secondary Schools*. Dunstable: Folens.

Eyre, D. (1997) *Able Children in Ordinary Schools*. London: David Fulton Publishers.

Eyre, D. and McClure, L. (eds) (2001) *Curriculum Provision for the Gifted and Talented in the Primary School: English, Maths, Science and ICT*. London: NACE/David Fulton Publishers.

Eyre, D. and Lowe, H. (eds) (2002) *Curriculum Provision for the Gifted and Talented in the Secondary School*. London: David Fulton Publishers.

* Freeman, J. (1998) *Educating the Very Able: Current International Research*. London: The Stationery Office.

Freeman, J. (2001) *Gifted Children Grown Up*. London: NACE/David Fulton Publishers.

George, D. (1995) *Gifted Education: Identification and Provision*. London: David Fulton Publishers.

House of Commons Education and Employment Committee (1999) Third Report: *Highly Able Children*, vols 1 and 2. London: HMSO.

Howe, M. J. A. (1990) *Sense and Nonsense About Hothouse Children*. Leicester: British Psychological Society.

Kent, G. (1996) *Teaching the Able Student*. Cambridge: Pearson.

Kirby, M. (1996) *Supporting the Able Student: A School Plan*. Cambridge: Pearson.

* Montgomery, D. (1996) *Educating the Able*. London: Cassell.

Reis, S. M., Burns, D. E. and Renzulli, J. S. (1994) *Curriculum Compacting: The Complete Guide to Modifying the Regular Curriculum for High Ability Students*. Victoria: Hawker Brownlow Education.

Sternberg, R. J. and Davidson, J. E. (eds) (1986) *Conceptions of Giftedness.* Cambridge: Cambridge University Press.

Sternberg, R. J. and Grigorenko, E. L. (2000) *Teaching for Successful Intelligence.* Arlington Heights, Ill.: Skylight.

Teare, B. (1997) *Effective Provision for Able and Talented Children.* Stafford: Network Educational Press.

Wallace, B. (2000) *Teaching the Very Able Child: Developing a Policy and Adopting Strategies for Provision.* London: NACE/David Fulton Publishers.

Webster, C. (1999) *Able and Gifted Children.* Dunstable: Folens.

Winebrenner, S. (1992) *Teaching Gifted Kids in the Regular Classroom: Strategies and Techniques Every Teacher can Use to Meet the Academic Needs of the Gifted and Talented.* Minneapolis, Minn.: Free Spirit.

Winner, E. (1996) *Gifted Children: Myths and Realities.* New York: Basic Books.

Learning styles and the brain

Buzan, T. and Buzan, B. (1995) *The Mindmap Book.* London: BBC Books.

Claxton, G. (1998) *Hare Brain Tortoise Mind: Why Intelligence Increases when you Think Less.* London: Fourth Estate.

* Claxton, G. (1999) *Wise Up: Learning to Live the Learning Life.* Stafford: Network Educational Press.

Dryden, G. and Vos, J. (1999) *The Learning Revolution: To Change the Way the World Learns.* Torrance, Calif.: The Learning Web.

Frender, G. (1990) *Learning to Learn: Strengthening Study Skills and Brain Power.* Nashville, Tenn.: Incentive.

Goleman, D. (1996) *Emotional Intelligence: Why It Can Matter More than IQ.* London: Bloomsbury.

Hart, S. (2000) *Thinking Through Teaching: A Framework for Enhancing Participation and Learning.* London: David Fulton Publishers.

Jensen, E. (1995) *The Learning Brain.* San Diego, Calif.: The Brain Store.

Watkins, C. *et al.* (1998) *Learning About Learning.* Warwick: NAPCE.

Watkins, C. (2001) 'Learning about learning enhances performance', *NSIN (National School Improvement Network) Research Matters*, **13**. London: Institute of Education.

Riding, R. and Rayner, S. (1998) *Cognitive Styles and Learning Strategies: Understanding Style Differences in Learning and Behaviour.* London: David Fulton Publishers.

Smith, A. (1996) *Accelerated Learning in the Classroom.* Stafford: Network Educational Press.

Smith, A. (1998) *Accelerated Learning in Practice: Brain-Based Methods for Accelerating Motivation and Achievement.* Stafford: Network Educational Press.

Smith, A. and Call, N. (1999) *The Alps Approach: Accelerated Learning in Primary Schools.* Stafford: Network Educational Press.

Local Education Authority publications

Cambridgeshire County Council LEA (1995) *Learning Now: The Cambridgeshire Experience of the High Ability Child.* Cambridge: Cambridgeshire County Council.

Cheshire County Council Education Services (1996) *Cheshire Management Guidelines: Identifying and Providing for Our Most Able Students.* Cheshire LEA.

City of Westminster (1996) *Working With Very Able Children: Parents and Teachers in Partnership.* London: City of Westminster.

* Hampshire Inspection and Advisory Service (2000) *Challenging Able Children: A Handbook for Primary Schools.* HIAS, tel. 01962 846549.

Kent County Council (1995) *Able Children: Guidance for Teachers, Parents and Governors on Supporting Very Able Children.* Kent Education Service.

Lincolnshire County Council (1999) *Effective Learning Training Materials.* Lincoln: Education and Cultural Services.

Northamptonshire County Council (1994) *The More Able Child: A Compendium of Ideas for Schools.* Northampton: NIAS.

Northumberland County Council (2001) *Thinking for Learning.* Northumberland: LEA Standards and Effectiveness Unit.

Worcestershire County Council (2000) Support Leaflets for Schools on Provision for More Able, Gifted and Talented Students. Worcestershire: Education Directorate Quality Division.

Multiple intelligences texts and resources

Bellanca, J. (1997) *Active Learning Handbook for the Multiple Intelligences Classroom.* Arlington Heights, Ill.: Skylight.

* Gardner, H. (1983) *Frames of Mind.* New York: Basic Books.

Gardner, H. (1993) *Multiple Intelligences: The Theory in Practice.* New York: Basic Books.

Gardner, H. (1997) *Extraordinary Minds.* London: Phoenix.

Gardner, H. (1999) *Intelligence Reframed: Multiple Intelligences for the 21st Century.* New York: Basic Books.

Haggerty, B. A. (1995) *Nurturing Intelligences: A Guide to Multiple Intelligences Theory and Teaching.* Menlow Park, Calif.: Addison-Wesley.

Lazear, D. (1991) *Seven Ways of Knowing: Teaching for Multiple Intelligences.* Arlington Heights, Ill.: Skylight.

Lazear, D. (1991) *Seven Ways of Teaching: The Artistry of Teaching with Multiple Intelligences.* Arlington Heights, Ill.: Skylight.

Lazear, D. (1994) *Seven Pathways of Learning: Teaching Students and Parents About Multiple Intelligences.* Tucson, Ariz.: Zephyr Press.

Lazear, D. (1994) *Multiple Intelligence Approaches to Assessment: Solving the Assessment Conundrum.* Tucson, Ariz.: Zephyr Press.

Marks-Tarlow, T. (1996) *Creativity Inside Out: Learning Through Multiple Intelligences.* Menlow Park, Calif.: Addison-Wesley.

Teacher Created Materials, Inc. (1999) *The Best of Multiple Intelligences.* Westminster, Calif.: Teacher Created Materials.

Philosophy for children and other thinking skills approaches

Adey, P. S., Shayer, M. and Yates, C. (2001) *Thinking Science: The Curriculum Materials of the CASE Project,* 3rd edn CD. Cheltenham: Nelson Thornes.

Burden, R. and Williams, M. (eds) (1998) *Thinking Through the Curriculum.* London: Routledge.

* Cam, P. (1995) *Thinking Together: Philosophical Inquiry for the Classroom.* Sydney, NSW: Hale and Iremonger.

Cam, P. (ed.) (1993) *Thinking Stories 1-3: Philosophical Inquiry for Children.* Alexandria, NSW: Hale and Iremonger.

Costello, P. J. M. (2000) *Thinking Skills and Early Childhood Education.* London: David Fulton Publishers.

Dawson, E. and Hymer, B. (2002) *Philosophy for Children: The Mirror of Erised* (**video**). Chelmsford: Multimedia Publications. Available from Still Thinking: email Stillthinkinguk@aol.com

Fisher, R. (1997) *Stories for Thinking.* Oxford: Nash Pollock. Also: *Games for Thinking* and *Poems for Thinking.*

* Fisher, R. (1998) *Teaching Thinking: Philosophical Enquiry in the Classroom.* London: Cassell.

Forte, I. and Schurr, S. (1996) *180 Icebreakers to Strengthen Critical Thinking and Problem-Solving Skills.* Nashville, Tenn.: Incentive.

Fox, R. (1996) *Thinking Matters: Stories to Encourage Thinking Skills.* Exmouth: Southgate.

Lake, M. and Needham, M. (undated) *Top Ten Thinking Tactics.* Birmingham: Questions Publishing Company.

Lake, M. and Needham, M. (2001) *Thinking with English*. Birmingham: Questions Publishing Company.

Law, S. (2000) *The Philosophy Files*. London: Orion.

Leat, D. (ed.) (1998) *Thinking Through Geography*. Cambridge: Chris Kington.

Leat, D. (ed.) (2002) *More Thinking Through Geography*. Cambridge: Chris Kington.

Matthews, G. B. (1980) *Philosophy and the Young Child*. Cambridge, Mass.: Harvard University Press.

McGuinness, C. (1999) *From Thinking Skills to Thinking Classrooms: A Review and Evaluation of Approaches for Developing Students' Thinking* (DfEE Research Report RR115). Nottingham: DfEE Publications.

Pofahl, J. (1996) *Creative and Critical Thinking* (activities). Grand Rapids, Mich.: T. S. Denison.

* Quinn, V. (1997) *Critical Thinking in Young Minds*. London: David Fulton Publishers.

Shayer, M., Johnson, D. and Adhami, M. (1998) *Thinking Maths: Accelerated Learning in Mathematics*. London: Heinemann.

* Wallace, B. (ed.) (2001) *Teaching Thinking Skills Across the Primary Curriculum: A Practical Approach for All Abilities*. London: NACE/David Fulton Publishers.

Warburton, N. (1999) *Philosophy: The Basics*. New York: Routledge.

Philosophy for children: outstanding picture-books for initial stimulus

Browne, A. (1997) *The Tunnel*. London: Walker Books. Other excellent P4C resources by the same author: *Zoo*; *Changes*; *Gorilla*; *Alice's Adventures in Wonderland*.

Burningham, J. (1978) *Would You Rather . . . ?* London: Jonathan Cape.

Foreman, M. (1974) *War and Peas*. London: Hamish Hamilton.

Hutchins, P. (1968) *Tom and Sam*. London: The Bodley Head. Other excellent P4C resources by the same author: *Clocks and More Clocks*; *The Very Worst Monster*; *You'll Soon Grow Into Them*; *Titch*.

Kroll, J. and James, A. (2000) *A Coat of Cats*. Bradfield, Essex: Happy Cat Books.

Marsden, J. and Tan, S. (1998) *The Rabbits*. Port Melbourne, Victoria: Lothian Books.

Oram, H. and Kitamura, S. (1984) *In the Attic*. London: Andersen Press.

Sheldon, D. and Blythe, G. (1993) *The Garden*. London: Hutchinson.

Silverstein, S. (1964) *The Giving Tree*. New York: Harper and Row.

Tilman, D. and Hsu, D. (2000) *Living Values: Values Activities for Children Ages 3–7 (and 8–14)*. New York: Living Values.

Trivizas, E. and Oxenbury, H. (1995) *The Three Little Wolves and the Big Bad Pig*. London: Mammoth.

Ungerer, T. (1998) *The Three Robbers*. Niwot, Colo.: Roberts Rinehart.

Wagner, J. and Brooks, R. (1979) *John Brown, Rose and the Midnight Cat*. Harmondsworth: Picture Puffin.

Wiesner, D. (1991) *Tuesday*. New York: Clarion Books.

Zolotow, C. and Vitale, S. (1995) *When the Wind Stops*. London: HarperCollins.

Social-emotional, spiritual and moral considerations

Bigger, S. and Brown, E. (1999) *Spiritual, Moral, Social and Cultural Education: Exploring Values in the Curriculum*. London: David Fulton Publishers.

Davis, G. A. (1996) *Teaching Values: An Idea Book for Teachers and Parents*. Cross Plains, Wis.: Westwood.

Day, J. (1994) *Creative Visualisation With Children: A Practical Guide*. Dorset: Element Books.

Freeman, J. (2001) *Gifted Children Grown Up*. London: NACE/David Fulton Publishers.

Goleman, D. (1996) *Emotional Intelligence: Why It Can Matter More than IQ*. London: Bloomsbury.

Heacox, D. (1991) *Up From Underachievement*. Minneapolis, Minn.: Free Spirit.

Hobday, A. and Ollier, K. (1998) *Creative Therapy: Activities with Children and Adolescents*. Leicester: British Psychological Society.

Lee-Corbin, H. and Denicolo, P. (1998) *Recognising and Supporting Able Children in Primary Schools*. London: David Fulton Publishers.

Lewis, B. A. (1998) *What Do You Stand For? A Kid's Guide to Building Character*. Minneapolis, Minn.: Free Spirit.

* Leyden, S. (1998) *Supporting the Child of Exceptional Ability at Home and School*, 2nd edn. London: NACE/David Fulton Publishers.

Montgomery, D. (ed.) (2000) *Able Underachievers*. London: Whurr.

Pomerantz, M. and Pomerantz, K. (2002) *Listening to Able Underachievers and Creating Opportunities for Change*. London: David Fulton Publishers.

Schmitz, C. C. and Galbraith, J. (1985) *Managing the Social and Emotional Needs of the Gifted: A Teacher's Survival Guide*. Minneapolis, Minn.: Free Spirit.

Steiner, M. (1993) *Learning from Experience: World Studies in the Primary Curriculum*. Stoke-on-Trent: Trentham Books.

Stone, M. K. (1995) *Don't Just Do Something – Sit There: Developing Children's Spiritual Awareness*. Norwich: Religious and Moral Education Press.

Stopper, M. J. (ed.) (2000) *Meeting the Social and Emotional Needs of Gifted and Talented Children*. London: NACE/David Fulton Publishers.

Winner, E. (1996) *Gifted Children: Myths and Realities*. New York: Basic Books.

Wood, A. and Richardson, R. (1992) *Inside Stories: Wisdom and Hope for Changing Worlds*. Stoke-on-Trent: Trentham Books.

Subject-specific (limited selection)

Adey, P. S., Shayer, M. and Yates, C. (2001) *Thinking Science: The Curriculum Materials of the CASE Project*, 3rd edn CD. Cheltenham: Nelson Thornes.

Bolt, B. (1982) *Mathematical Activities* (also: *More Mathematical Activities* and *Even More Mathematical Activities*). Cambridge: Cambridge University Press.

Dean, G. (1998) *Challenging the More Able Language User*. London: NACE/David Fulton Publishers.

Dean, M. (2000) *Questions Literacy Resources: Bill's New Frock by Anne Fine*. Birmingham: Questions Publishing Company.

Ernst, B. (1985) *The Magic Mirror of M. C. Escher*. Diss: Tarquin.

Eyre, D. and McClure, L. (eds) (2001) *Curriculum Provision for the Gifted and Talented in the Primary School : English, Maths, Science and ICT*. London: NACE/David Fulton Publishers.

Fielker, D. (1997) *Extending Mathematical Ability Through Whole Class Teaching*. London: Hodder and Stoughton.

Gardiner, A. (2000) *Acceleration or Enrichment: Serving the Needs of the Top 10% in Mathematics*. Birmingham: University of Birmingham School of Mathematics.

Gardiner, A. (ed.) (2000) *Maths Challenge (1-3)*. Oxford: Oxford University Press.

Kennard, R. (1996) *Teaching Mathematically Able Children*. Oxford: NACE.

Koshy, V. (2001) *Teaching Mathematics to Able Children*. London: David Fulton Publishers.

Lake, M. and Needham, M. (2001) *Thinking with English*. Birmingham: Questions Publishing Company.

O'Brien, P. (1998) *Teaching Scientifically Able Students in the Secondary School*. Oxford: NACE. (Also by the same author and publisher: *Teaching Scientifically Able Students in the Primary School*.)

Ross, L. (2000) *Questions Literacy Resources: The Story of Tracy Beaker by Jacqueline Wilson*. Birmingham: Questions Publishing Company.

Straker, A. (1993) *Talking Points in Mathematics*. Cambridge: Cambridge University Press.

Young children

Freeman, J. (1991) *How To Raise a Bright Child: Practical Ways to Encourage Your Child's Talents from 0–5 Years*. London: Vermilion.

Griffin, N. S., Curtiss, J., McKenzie, J., Maxfield, L. and Crawford, M. (1995) 'Authentic assessment of able children using a regular classroom observation protocol', *Flying High* (former title for the NACE journal) (Spring 1995): 34–42.

Hyams, S. M. (1989) *Challenges for Children: Problem-Solving for Young Children*. Colchester: Claire.

Micklethwait, L. (1994) *I Spy: Animals in Art*. London: HarperCollins.

* Porter, L. (1999) *Gifted Young Children: A Guide for Teachers and Parents*. Buckingham: Open University Press.

Smutny, J. F., Walker, S. Y. and Meckstroth, E. A. (1997) *Teaching Young Gifted Children in the Regular Classroom: Identifying, Nurturing and Challenging Ages 4–9*. Minneapolis, Minn.: Free Spirit.

Wick, W. and Marzollo, J. (1992) *I Spy: A Book of Picture Riddles*. London: Scholastic.

References

Barrow Community Learning Partnership (BCLP) (2001) *Year Two Action Plan*. Barrow: BCLP.

Bellanca, J. (1997) *Active Learning Handbook for the Multiple Intelligences Classroom*. Arlington Heights, Ill.: Skylight.

Black, P. and Wiliam, D. (1998) *Inside the Black Box: Raising Standards through Classroom Assessment*. London: King's College School of Education.

Bloom, B. S. (ed.) (1956) *Taxonomy of Educational Objectives*, vol. 1. London: Longman.

Boring, E. G. (1923) 'Intelligence as the tests test it', *New Republic* (6 June 1923): 35–7.

Boud, D. J. (1995) *Enhancing Learning Through Self-Assessment*. London: Kogan Page.

Boud, D. J. and Walker, D. (1990) 'Making the most of experience', *Studies in Continuing Education* **12**(2):61–80.

Boud, D. J., Keogh, R. and Walker, D. (1985) 'Promoting reflection in learning a model', in Boud, D. J., Keogh, R. and Walker, D. (eds), *Reflection: Turning Experience into Learning*. London: Kogan Page.

Ceci, S. (1990) *On Intelligence . . . More or Less: A Bio-ecological Treatise on Intellectual Development*. Englewood Cliffs, N.J.: Prentice Hall.

Ceci, S. (1996) *On Intelligence*. Cambridge, Mass.: Harvard University Press.

Cheshire County Council Education Services (1996) *Cheshire Management Guidelines: Identifying and Providing for Our Most Able Students*. Cheshire: LEA.

Claxton, G. (1999) *Wise Up: Learning to Live the Learning Life*. Stafford: Network Educational Press.

Csikszentmihalyi, M. (1996) *Creativity*. New York: HarperCollins.

Eyre, D. (2001) 'An effective primary school for the gifted and talented', in Eyre, D. and McClure, L. (eds) *Curriculum Provision for the Gifted and Talented in the Primary School: English, Maths, Science and ICT*. London: NACE/David Fulton Publishers.

Eyre, D. and McClure, L. (eds) (2001) *Curriculum Provision for the Gifted and Talented in the Primary School: English, Maths, Science and ICT*. London: NACE/David Fulton Publishers.

Fisher, R. (1998) *Teaching Thinking: Philosophical Enquiry in the Classroom*. London: Cassell.

Freeman, J. (1979) *Gifted Children*. Lancaster: MTP Press.

Freeman, J. (1991a) *Gifted Children Growing Up*. London: Cassell.

Freeman, J. (1991b) *How To Raise a Bright Child: Practical Ways to Encourage your Child's Talents from 0–5 Years*. London: Vermilion.

Freeman, J. (1998) *Educating the Very Able: Current International Research*. London: The Stationery Office.

Freeman, J. (2001) *Gifted Children Grown Up*. London: NACE/David Fulton Publishers.

Gardiner, A. (2000) *Acceleration or Enrichment: Serving the Needs of the Top 10% in Mathematics*. Birmingham: University of Birmingham School of Mathematics.

Gardner, H. (1983) *Frames of Mind*. New York: Basic Books.

Gardner, H. (1993) *Multiple Intelligences: The Theory in Practice*. New York: Basic Books.

Gardner, H. (1997) *Extraordinary Minds*. London: Phoenix.

Gardner, H. (1999) *Intelligence Reframed: Multiple Intelligences for the 21st Century*. New York: Basic Books.

Geake, J. G. (2002) 'Knock down the fences: implications of brain science for education', National Association for Able Children in Education (NACE) *Newsletter*, (Spring): 4–7, reprinted from *Primary Matters*, (April 2000): 41–3.

Goleman, D. (1996) *Emotional Intelligence: Why it can Matter More Than IQ*. London: Bloomsbury.

Goodhew, G. (2001) 'Homework: getting it right', *Special Children* (Nov./Dec.): 16–17.

Gowen, J. C. and Demos, G. D. (1964) *The Education and Guidance of the Ablest*. Springfield, Ill.: Charles C. Thomas.

Griffin, N. S., Curtiss, J., McKenzie, J., Maxfield, L. and Crawford, M. (1995) 'Authentic assessment of able children using a regular classroom observation protocol', *Flying High* (former title for the NACE journal) (Spring 1995), 34–42.

Haggerty, B. A. (1995) *Nurturing Intelligences: A Guide to Multiple Intelligences Theory and Teaching*. Menlow Park, Calif.: Addison-Wesley.

Hart, S. (2000) *Thinking Through Teaching: A Framework for Enhancing Participation and Learning*. London: David Fulton Publishers.

Hazlewood, P., Bayliss, V. and Hargreaves, D. (2002) 'Opening minds: towards a 21st century curriculum', National Association for Able Children in Education (NACE) *Newsletter*, (Spring): 14–20, reprinted from *RSA Journal* (4 April 2001).

Herrnstein, R. and Murray, C. (1994) *The Bell Curve: Intelligence and Class Structure in American Life*. New York: Free Press.

House of Commons Education and Employment Committee (1999) Third Report: *Highly Able Children*, vols 1 and 2. London: HMSO.

Howe, M. J. A. (1990) *Sense and Nonsense About Hothouse Children*. Leicester: British Psychological Society.

Hymer, B., Michel, D. and Todd, E. (2002) 'Dynamic consultation: towards process and challenge', *Educational Psychology in Practice*, **18**(1):47–62.

Kerry, T. (2001) 'Managing the learning of able students', *Educating Able Children*, **5**(2):4–11.

Koshy, V. and Casey, R. (2000) *Special Abilities Scales: Observational Assessment for Identifying Able and High-Potential Students*. London: Hodder and Stoughton.

Lazear, D. (1994a) *Seven Pathways of Learning: Teaching Students and Parents About Multiple Intelligences*. Tucson, Ariz.: Zephyr Press.

Lazear, D. (1994b) *Multiple Intelligence Approaches to Assessment: Solving the Assessment Conundrum*. Tucson, Ariz.: Zephyr Press.

Light, P. and Littleton, K. (1999) *Social Processes in Children's Learning*, Cambridge Studies in Cognitive and Perceptual Development. Cambridge: Cambridge University Press.

Marks-Tarlow, T. (1996) *Creativity Inside Out: Learning Through Multiple Intelligences*. Menlow Park, Calif.: Addison-Wesley.

McGuinness, C. (1999) *From Thinking Skills to Thinking Classrooms: A Review and Evaluation of Approaches for Developing Students' Thinking* (DfEE Research Report RR115). Nottingham: DfEE Publications.

Mönks, F. J. (1992) 'Development of gifted children: the issues of identification and programming', in Monks, F. J. and Peters, W. (eds) *Talent for the Future*. Assen/Maastricht: Van Gorcum.

Montgomery, D. (1996) *Educating the Able*. London: Cassell.

Montgomery, D. (ed.) (2000) *Able Underachievers*. London: Whurr.

Office for Standards in Education(Ofsted) (2001) *Providing for Gifted and Talented Students: An Evaluation of Excellence in Cities and Other Grant-Funded Programmes*. London: Ofsted; www.ofsted.gov.uk.

O'Hara, M. (2002) 'Anyone know a good plumber?', The Saturday *Guardian*, Jobs and Money Supplement, 9 March 2002: 2–3.

Ollerton, M. (2001) 'Inclusion and entitlement, equality of opportunity and quality of curriculum provision', *Support for Learning: British Journal of Learning Support*, **16**:35–40.

Reis, S. M., Burns, D. E. and Renzulli, J. S. (1994) *Curriculum Compacting: The Complete Guide to Modifying the Regular Curriculum for High Ability Students*. Victoria: Hawker Brownlow Education.

Renzulli, J. S. (1977) *The Enrichment Triad Model: A Guide for Developing Defensible Programs for the Gifted and Talented*. Mansfield Conn.: Creative Learning Press.

Renzulli, J. S. (1990) 'A practical system for identifying gifted and talented students', *Early Child Development and Care*, **63**:9–18.

Robinson, N. M. (2000) 'Giftedness in very young children: how seriously should it be taken?', in Friedman, R. C. and Shore, B. M. (eds) *Talents Unfolding: Cognition and Development*. Washington DC: American Psychological Association.

Rowley, S. (1995) 'Identification and development of talent in young athletes', in Freeman, J., Span, P. and Wagner, H. (eds), *Actualising Talent: A Lifelong Challenge*. London: Cassell.

Sternberg, R. J. (1986) 'A triarchic theory of intelligence', in Sternberg, R. J. and Davidson, J. E. (eds), *Conceptions of Giftedness*. Cambridge: Cambridge University Press.

Sternberg, R. J. (1997) 'The concept of intelligence and its role in lifelong learning and success', *American Psychologist*, **52**:1030–7.

Sternberg, R. J. (2000) 'Wisdom as a form of giftedness', *Gifted Child Quarterly*, **44**:252–60.

Sternberg, R. J. and Grigorenko, E. L. (2000) *Teaching for Successful Intelligence*. Arlington Heights, Ill.: Skylight.

Stevens, A. (1980) *Clever Children in Comprehensive Schools*. London: Penguin.

Stone, M. K. (1995) *Don't Just Do Something – Sit There: Developing Children's Spiritual Awareness*. Norwich: Religious and Moral Education Press.

Stoppard, M. (1995) *Complete Baby and Childcare*. London: Dorling Kindersley.

Teacher Created Materials, Inc. (1999) *The Best of Multiple Intelligences*. Westminster, Calif.: Teacher Created Materials.

Terman, L. M. (1925) *Genetic Studies of Genius*, Vol. 1: *Mental and Physical Traits of a Thousand Gifted Children*. Stanford, Calif.: Stanford University Press.

Treffinger, D. J. and Feldhusen, J. F. (1996) 'Talent recognition and development: successor to gifted education', *Journal for the Education of the Gifted*, **19**:181–93.

UNESCO (1994) *Salamanca Statement on Special Needs Education*. Paris: UNESCO. www.unesco.org/education/educprog/sne/salamanc/index/htm

Wallace, B. (2000) *Teaching the Very Able Child: Developing a Policy and Adopting Strategies for Provision*. London: NACE/David Fulton Publishers.

Warwick, I. (2001) 'Providing for under-achieving students using Renzulli's type III enrichment activities: gifted and talented video projects at Holland Park comprehensive school', *Gifted Education International*, **16**:29–42.

Watkins, C. (2001) 'Learning about learning enhances performance', *NSIN (National School Improvement Network) Research Matters*, No. 13. London: Institute of Education.

Wenger, W. (1998) *Communities of Practice: Learning Meaning and Identity*. Cambridge: Cambridge University Press.

Winner, E. (1996) *Gifted Children: Myths and Realities*. New York: Basic Books.

Zorman, R. (1998) 'A model for adolescent giftedness identification via challenges (MAGIC)', *Gifted and Talented International*, **13**:65–72.

Index